Beyond Nuclear Thinking

Beyond Nuclear Thinking

ROBERT W. MALCOLMSON

McGill-Queen's University Press
Montreal & Kingston • London • Buffalo

© McGill-Queen's University Press 1990
ISBN 0–7735–0784–1 (cloth)
ISBN 0–7735–0802–3 (paper)

Legal deposit fourth quarter 1990
Bibliothèque nationale du Québec

Printed in Canada on acid-free paper

This book has been published with the help of a
grant from the Canada Council and the assistance of
the School of Graduate Studies and Research at
Queen's University.

Canadian Cataloguing in Publication Data

Malcolmson, Robert W
    Beyond nuclear thinking
    Includes bibliographical references.
    ISBN 0-7735-0784-1 (bound) –
    ISBN 0-7735-0802-3 (pbk).
    1. World politics – 1945–   . 2. Deterrence
    (Strategy).   I. Title.
    JX1974.7.M38 1990   327.1   C90-090324-4

This book was printed in Palatino 10/12 on 2506 picas
by Typo Litho composition inc.

For Edward Thompson
an exceptional teacher

Contents

Preface

Most of what is written about nuclear weapons is focused on the here and now. This present-centredness is understandable: after all, debates go on, claims and counter-claims are uttered, evidence is constantly being sifted and assessed, and decisions have to be made. However, this focus on the present is constricting, sometimes seriously so, both for our understanding of the nuclear age and for the exercise of thoughtful political judgment. To be confined intellectually in the political present, to be too much absorbed in the immediacies of the moment, precludes a proper appreciation of the politics and culture of our age of weapons of mass destruction. The nuclear age has a past that is full and substantial and no longer all that short. This is a past that has given shape to the objective realities of the 1990s (weapons systems, war plans, strategic doctrines, and the like) and to what citizens take to be and think about these realities. A formidable legacy has been passed on, and whatever one's opinions and personal feelings, it will have to be in some sense borne with and managed, preferably intelligently and responsibly. All the more important, then, to understand what we have inherited and why people in the recent past thought about nuclear weapons in the way that they did.

This is not then a book about current affairs, and its principal messages are little affected by the torrent of East-West political events that began in the late 1980s. Many of these events were seen as encouraging and as sources of optimism, and certainly those who made them were hopeful that their lives would get better. But these momentous developments, most of them in eastern and central Europe, had little impact on many of the basic facts of life in the nuclear age. As some lethal hardware was dismantled, new weapons were deployed and newer ones still were on the drawing board. Established nuclear strategies persisted; military doctrines were modified (if at all) only at the margins; the proliferation of nuclear weapons and ballistic missiles (mostly outside Europe) seemed imminent; and the verb "to deter" remained central to the liturgies of those who spoke in the name of national or Western or even international security. A deeply rooted history of nuclearized thinking remained actively at work. This thinking was highly resistant to fundamental change, unlike real political relations; indeed, in many respects these dogmas and the entrenched interests that promoted them were self-sustaining and self-legitimating and largely unmoved by the actual dynamics of international politics. Large bureaucracies like to define truth in their own way. Those associated with nuclear weapons have been no exception.

Thus, even as the Cold War was declared to be ending, much of its lethal baggage persisted with vigour. This was military baggage that had been accumulating for half a century; it was embedded in various political systems; and there was no way that it could be easily or quickly jettisoned, even assuming the will to do so. Here was a heavy burden of history that could not be evaded. Sometimes the centrality of the nuclear threat receded in the public conscious-ness, as it had during the 1970s and seemed again to recede from 1989 as the East Bloc unravelled. But the nuclear threat, which is objectively central to modern world history, cannot be downgraded merely by virtue of people feeling better. Feelings are only a part of security. Objectively, the world of the 1990s continues to be inhab-ited by political scorpions, the great nation-states, whose leaderships possess extraordinary destructive powers. These scorpions still con-front the problem (as they have for years) of how to manage and control their mutually poisonous powers; or, alternately, in the eyes of some of the weapons' keepers, how to use these powers threat-eningly, and unilaterally, in the interest of the sovereign state. The perils and dilemmas of the nuclear age are sure to be much more enduring than the animosities of the Cold War.

Academic discourse about nuclear weapons has been commonly esoteric and inward-looking. This book, by contrast, presents a broadly conceived and non-technical interpretation of life and thought in the nuclear age. It tries to stick to fundamentals and not to become absorbed in arcane details of technology and strategic doctrine, the importance of which has been chronically overvalued. Perhaps in the 1990s we should think of ourselves as having lived through the first chapter of the nuclear age, with many more chap-ters to follow, possibly with – but we hope without – catastrophic violence. This first chapter of the nuclear age, the period since 1945, does not decisively determine the story that will follow. It only sets the stage for a future that could unfold in many different ways. But the setting for any story is important; and in moving into the future there is nothing to be gained from having poor memories. Remembering the past is essential; and adequate remembering demands sustained, disciplined, and independent enquiry. "The past," said William Faulkner, "is never dead. It's not even past." *Beyond Nuclear Thinking* has been composed with this sentiment in mind.

Thinking historically: this is one central concern of this book. Its other is to think critically. While it might be said that one should always think critically, eschewing dogma and clichés and facile answers, critical thinking is particularly important when trying to come to grips with military science because so much of the apparently informed discussion of nuclear weapons has been paid for, or promoted, or at least significantly shaped by the possessors of these weapons. Needless to say, their views are not disinterested. Certain questions get shunted aside; orthodoxies take root and are perpetuated by those with an interest in sustaining them; some of the questionable decisions and policies of the past are conveniently forgotten or explained away; propaganda and disinformation sometimes intrude into scholarship; and national identities and partisanship (not to mention patriotic zeal) commonly taint the perspectives of those who offer themselves as "defence intellectuals." This is not to say that these sources have had nothing worthwhile or sensible to say. They are, however, laden with self-justification; and they tend to be particularly concerned to rationalize the world as it has become. In this professional culture of shared assumptions and approved opinions, alternative perspectives have not been warmly welcomed and, whenever possible, have been dismissed as of little concern to anyone save the innocents in the peace movement. Serious men and women, it has been assumed, are realists who know how power politics actually works and are not taken in by visionary ideals and naïve illusions.

The title of this book is perhaps misleading in one respect, for my focus is largely on American military science and especially American thinking about nuclear weapons since the end of World War II. This emphasis is partly a function of the availability and accessibility of sources: not surprisingly, Americans, as citizens of the first and for many years foremost nuclear nation, have written a lot about nuclear weapons. The United States has produced some of the most thoughtful strategic writers and the richest body of specialist literature on this subject; and these discussions and analyses, though often classified and at least partly restricted, have been more open to public scrutiny than those in any other nuclear state. But there is another and more important reason for this book's emphasis on the United States: in the nuclear age, the United States has almost always been the leading nation in military science. It has usually been on the cutting edge of weapons developments, especially with respect to nuclear weapons. In this field, with rare exceptions, it has set the pace and the technological standards, which other states might or might not then choose to follow and emulate. The Soviet Union usually tried to do so. But in military science it has played a largely reactive role; innovations and breakthroughs in military hardware have come largely from the United States. In fact, it has been a recurrent refrain in American military-industrial circles that the alleged large Soviet quantitative advantages could only be offset by continued improvement in the quality of American weaponry. For many years, Moscow was certainly the initiating political force in eastern and parts of central Europe and, on occasion, in power vacuums and revolutionary upheavals that cropped up elsewhere in the globe. The initiatives of the United States were more obviously technological in character. Its most remarkable initiative in World War II had been the secret Manhattan Project, which created the world's first atomic bombs; and among the initiatives favoured by Washington from the late 1940s, the nuclear threat, usually spoken of as "our deterrent," and refinements on and enhancements of this threat, were very much at the centre of American thinking about their own and the world's security and about how to preserve peace on a turbulent planet.

My intellectual debts in preparing this book are mostly to various experts and other authors, whose ideas and arguments I have drawn upon freely. I have tried to acknowledge these debts at appropriate places in the endnotes. These notes also include references to many of the relevant primary historical sources: official reports, political statements, military doctrines, strategic commentaries, journalistic opinion, interpretative reflections, and the like. As much as seems proper in a short study, I have allowed these primary sources opportunities to speak for themselves. Several colleagues and friends have taken the trouble to read all or parts of the manuscript and offer helpful comments and criticisms, notably Charles Pentland, Geoffrey Pearson, Donald Akenson, Kevin Leppmann, and Patricia Malcolmson. Two readers for McGill-Queen's University Press also pressed me to make a number of improvements that I would not otherwise have considered. Passages of this book appeared previously in two essays, one published in the *Queen's Quarterly*, the other in *Peace and Security*, the quarterly magazine of the Canadian Institute for International Peace and Security. A grant from the Advisory Research Committee at Queen's University helped to support my studies in 1988–9. Yvonne Place was responsible for efficiently producing an accurate typescript, and Marion Magee edited the manuscript in an admirably constructive manner. Finally, I intend this book's dedication as a small gesture of appreciation for the intellectual guidance rendered over many years by a remarkable historian whose exemplary commitment and generosity, discipline and probing criticism, I have had the good fortune to be able to benefit from.

February 1990   RWM

The scientific revolution ... changes not the power relations within mankind, but the very background of human existence, the scenery against which the drama of history will unfold.

Eugene Rabinowitch,
Bulletin of the Atomic Scientists, December 1962

CHAPTER ONE

"The Great Deterrent"

The day is coming when the quantity of atomic weapons we are capable of making could be sufficient, beyond any question, to serve as the paramount instrument of victory. There is virtually no limit and no limiting factor upon the number of A-bombs which the United States can manufacture, given time and given a decision to proceed all-out ... I propose that we make our best and cheapest weapon – the atomic weapon – the real backbone of our peace power.

Senator Brien E. McMahon, chairman of the Joint Congressional Committee on Atomic Energy, 18 September 1951[1]

In 1957, a marshal of the Royal Air Force, Sir John Slessor, published a collection of his essays and lectures under the title, *The Great Deterrent*. These words were apt and entirely in accord with the conventional Anglo-American thinking of the early and mid-1950s. For they drew attention to a fundamental premise of Western politico-military policy: nuclear weaponry had become critically important, in the opinion of its non-communist possessors, to the pursuit of peace and security. The bomb (first, fission; later, fusion) was seen as the crucial counterweight to the aggressive instincts of world communism. It was first and foremost the bomb – the free world's bomb – that would prevent a major war from breaking out. The bomb was seen as a peacekeeper or, more accurately, as *the* peacekeeper. As Slessor wrote in another book at this time: "I believe ... that the hydrogen bomb in the armouries of the world brings a message not of despair but of hope – hope and even confidence that no one will ever again resort to major war as an instrument of policy."[2] Atomic air power, he thought, "is ... the real preventive of war": "the continued existence of atomic weapons gives us an almost certain chance of preventing another world war."[3]

The idea that the bomb could serve to keep the peace was certainly not new. Harry Truman had been perhaps the first prominent public figure to suggest this possibility. On 6 August 1945, at the conclusion of the radio address that announced the destruction of Hiroshima, the president spoke of determining, in the future, "how atomic power can become a powerful and forceful influence towards the maintenance of world peace."[4] Given the widespread belief in peace through strength, and given the assumption that the atomic bomb was an expression of strength, it was not long before the bomb and the prevention of war came to be closely linked in the public mind. Western security would be based on the destructive capabilities of air power. This power to destroy was seen, of course, as strictly defensive. It was designed, people said, solely to deal with aggression: to dissuade a potential aggressor and to punish an actual aggressor. The conception of strength that came to predominate was well enunciated a couple of years after Hiroshima by a special Presidential Commission on Air Policy. The commission reported its belief "that a strong United States will be a force for peace. Our armaments will not guarantee that peace absolutely. But the chances of avoiding a war will be greatly increased if this country has the available force to strike back and to defeat anyone who breaks the peace. A strong United States will be welcomed by all peace-loving nations. The countries who want to live under regimes of freedom will see in our armaments not a threat but an assurance."[5]

These beliefs, which flourished during those years when the United States enjoyed a monopoly in atomic weapons and thus could threaten without being threatened in kind, proved to be remarkably resilient. Nuclear weapons were called upon to sustain the American role of global policeman. As the Cold War intensified from 1948, increasing reliance was placed on the alleged deterrent power of weapons of mass destruction and on their presumed value in restraining and perhaps combating communism. As the British minister of defence put it in September 1948, in a letter to the American secretary of defense: "The atomic weapon is the greatest single source of military strength in the world at present, and it is in the interests of the security of the United States, as well as that of the United Kingdom, that both countries should develop it to the maximum of their ability, and with all possible speed."[6] (The Americans were less keen on the idea of a British atomic bomb.)

Communism, it was agreed, had to be contained; containment, from the late 1940s on, was increasingly construed in terms of military might (as distinct from political and economic vitality); and the most robust and least troublesome bulwark of freedom was said to be the deterrent power of atomic weapons. The goal was becoming clear: create a healthy fear in Moscow of American destructive power, and by means of this fear keep communism in line (at a minimum) or even roll it back (a larger ambition). An early proponent of this view had been General Leslie Groves, the military commander of the Manhattan Project that had designed and manufactured the first atomic bombs. In his customary blunt manner, Groves had stated in a memorandum of January 1946 what he saw to be the requirements for American security: "If there are to be atomic weapons in the world, we must have the best, the biggest and the most." Groves's views, we now know, had a substantial impact on American security policy during the immediate postwar years.[7]

Atomic weapons, then, came to be widely regarded as the vital factor in the conduct of Cold War diplomacy. Rather than arguing for any particular restraint in the face of their destructive power (at least in public), American policy-makers came to think largely in terms of their utility and of the messages of strength they would convey to Moscow. A strong America was coming to mean a heavily nuclearized America. The nuclear arsenal of the United States was to be the centrepiece of its national security policy. Even after the Soviet Union joined the nuclear club in August 1949, to the surprise and consternation of American leaders, there was no rethinking of official policy. Indeed, with the decision in 1950 to develop the H-bomb, the stakes were increased. Although the monopoly might be lost, it was argued, a decisive predominance could be maintained. As an official in the State Department put it in January 1950 (and this was a widely shared opinion): "I assume that we can maintain a wide superiority in atomic weapons over the Soviet Union, probably for an indefinite period of time."[8]

Such superiority in atomic air power was thought to be essential to United States national security. Thomas Finletter, a former secretary of the United States Air Force (USAF), made this point forcefully in 1954: "Much of our diplomatic strength in recent years has come from our obviously overwhelming superiority in atomic weapons. Nothing but weakness will come from losing it." He spoke of the mid-1950s as "a time when the survival of the country calls on us to be vigilant as we never have been before in maintaining our air-atomic supremacy over the Russians."[9] (It is noteworthy, however, and perhaps a sign of doubt and alternative sensitivities, that in the same sentence Finletter referred to his age as "a time when science has made war truly incompatible with civilization.") Vigilance, supremacy, staying ahead: these were the watchwords of this brief era of Pax Americana. Referring to the long-range bomber and atomic weapons in a speech of October 1954, James H. Douglas, under secretary of the USAF between 1953 and 1957, was thankful "for our superiority in these weapons that we have taken the leadership in developing. For without them our world position would today be perilous indeed. More than any other single element of national strength, air power has preserved such peace as we have known during the past decade."[10] Thomas E. Murray, a member of the Atomic Energy Commission between 1950 and 1957, thought of the late 1940s as a time "when America's atomic potential was almost its sole defense against Soviet aggression." Atomic energy, he asserted, was "that one force on which the security of America and the Free World rests."[11] This view would continue to be reiterated by officials and strategic experts and popular commentators. Air-atomic superiority was "a decisive element – very possibly *the* decisive element – in the postwar security of the United States and the free world."[12]

Public discourse in the 1950s was replete with these assumptions (and they were very much assumptions, for they could be neither proven nor disproven). In 1955, for example, the May issue of the *Annals of the American Academy of Political and Social Science* was devoted to the theme of "Air Power and National Security," and the foreword to this volume by Robert Strausz-Hupé, a prominent student of geopolitics, offered reflections on nuclear weapons that were already widely held. "Inevitably," he said, "in an atomic age, nuclear air power must be the sword and shield of freedom ... Without American air power, postwar Europe might have fallen an easy prey to Communism. Without this same power it would have been difficult, if not impossible, to forge the system of alliances uniting most of the world's peaceful and democratic nations. Atomic air power has given the free world a true and trusted defense." Long-range air power meant that the Soviet heartland was no longer invulnerable; consequently, all important communist military assets, no matter how remote, could be destroyed in a retaliatory nuclear attack. The "aggressor," then, had no sanctuary from which to launch a surprise attack, and thus, it was hoped, aggression would be effectively deterred – deterred by the fear of the striking power of the West. As Strausz-Hupé put it: "The American nuclear force for years has been pointed at the very core of incipient aggression. The free world's plan is to continue to employ American and British nuclear superiority as the chief deterrent to cataclysmic folly."[13]

American policy towards the Soviet Union was, in short, premised on the continued existence of American air superiority. Command of the air was seen as both essential and feasible. Air power, according to Stefan Possony in a book published in 1949 by the Infantry Journal Press, "must be the guardian of liberty and progress. The global air dominion must be held securely by a technically superior ... United States Air Force of overwhelming bombing and fire power ... The dominion of the air exercised to preserve peace and to lead the forces of freedom to victory is the key to mankind's better future."[14] This supremacy would make it possible, in the eyes of most leading strategists, to destroy the Soviet Union's war-making capacity without fear that it could destroy the military assets of the United States. Soviet territory was exposed to crippling air attack in a way that the American homeland was not. If war were to break out as a result of Soviet aggression (which was assumed to be the only plausible cause of war), air power would pave the way to victory. Dale O. Smith, a USAF brigadier general, presented the case for victory through air power in a book published in 1955 (which had been officially cleared for publication). In the event of war, he argued: "Once we have achieved air dominance, the enemy has no recourse but to surrender. It would not be necessary to wipe out all his cities to convince him of this. The obvious capability to do this during a state of total war should be sufficient to force him to terms. But suppose he is stubborn and continues to advance with his surface forces. What then? Then we shall be obliged to lay on a massive air siege. Punitive air action can be directed against his national resources until he comes to terms." As he remarked elsewhere, "No power can be *too* destructive in *absolute* war."[15]

Here, then, was the public position of the United States in the face of the communist menace. The threat to freedom was extraordinary; so too must be the means of defence. Air-atomic power was and had already been shown to be indispensable to the free world's security. As one authority asserted toward the end of the 1950s: "The posture of American air forces to wage all-out war, if forced upon the West by Communist aggression, has served to maintain the world balance of power, albeit an uneasy one."[16] Without nuclear weapons, the scales would have tipped dangerously, perhaps disastrously, in favour of the Kremlin and its tyranny. Security through air power, a doctrine that had it roots in the years between the two world wars, was a central theme in the political culture of the 1950s. Although this nuclear-centred policy did not go unchallenged, the critics were always in a minority and had little impact on decision-making or weapons procurement. A retired brigadier general, Bonner Fellers, championed "this new and most potent war deterrent," the bomber wedded to the atomic bomb, in a book published in 1953, entitled *Wings for Peace*. The deterrent, he said, "will free our Allies to go about their normal pursuits with confidence in the future" – an early expression of the notion of the "nuclear umbrella." Fellers concluded his advocacy with the assurance that "the free world can survive the deadly total Red threat if we man our air ramparts and stand by with atomic weapons. Can anyone say," he asked, "that these secrets of creation were not entrusted to man by his Creator to be used first to deter war and ultimately to promote peace and good will?"[17] These were simply different, more moralistic words for Slessor's great deterrent. Nuclear weaponry should be seen, not as a potential destroyer of civilization, but as a destroyer of war itself.

EMBRACING THE BOMB

During the postwar years in the United States, there was a dramatic reworking of the political agenda of fear. Immediately after Hiroshima, public consciousness was focused on fear of the bomb itself and on the new weapon's implications for security in the future. The peril of the bomb was widely discussed, especially by intellectuals and journalists, and its frightening significance for the world's future was pondered at length, notably during late 1945 and 1946. By the end of the 1940s, however, this fear had been largely swept aside, to be replaced by the fear of communism. The real threat to civilization, it came to be believed, was not nuclear weaponry but Soviet barbarism – this of course was the era of militant Stalinism – and the Soviet quest for world domination. Paul Boyer, in a major study of nuclear consciousness during these years, has drawn attention to the orthodoxies that had become dominant by 1950. The fears and warnings of just a few years before had come to be seen as excessive, alarmist, and unwarranted. The bomb, it was now said, "was not so bad after all, and in any event it was here to stay. The duty of the good citizen was to come to terms with it, and the best way to do that was to show enthusiasm for the peaceful atom and support civil defense."[18] The challenge facing Americans was to learn how to cope with nuclear war, should it come, and to concentrate on dealing with the insidious evil of communism. The "terrible weapon" of 1945–6 – in the words of Robert Oppenheimer, the wartime director of the Los Alamos laboratory, in late 1945 – had become, as Boyer puts it, "the shield of the Republic by 1950; America must have as many nuclear weapons as possible, and the bigger the better, for the death struggle with communism that lay ahead."[19]

In this new climate of fear, the bomb itself was no longer such a fearful thing. Consider, for example, a mundane incident that nicely reveals something of the changing political mood. In September 1950 the *New York Times* reported that a record of a song entitled "Old Man Atom," which had been composed by a Los Angeles news-paperman shortly after Hiroshima, was being withdrawn from distribution by R.C.A. Victor and Columbia Records, apparently because "pressure had been brought on them on the ground that the song followed the Communist party 'peace line'." The message of the song, which had previously been entitled "Talking Atomic Blues," was said to be that "the atomic bomb endangers all people everywhere and that we must have peace in the world or we will all be in pieces." This message was unacceptable to influential pressure groups who argued that the song "parroted the Communist line on peace and reflected the propaganda for the Stockholm 'peace petition'" and thus should not be available for public consumption.[20] Learning to Love the Bomb: this flippant phrase of the time embodied a measure of truth. In an April 1954 editorial, "Facing Up to the Bomb," the *New York Times* gave voice to what by then was a commonplace opinion: "Though Soviet Russia has mastered the secret of both atomic and hydrogen explosions, the United States and through it all free nations have the lead at present in the production of atomic and hydrogen weapons, and this fact increases the strength of the free world and therewith the chances of world peace."[21] Satisfaction was expressed about the possession of this superior destructive power.

This shift towards explicitly pro-nuclear thinking helped to liberate nuclear weapons from previous political constraints. In the early 1950s civilian controls were relaxed, and bombs were placed directly in the hands of military commanders (the civilian Atomic Energy Commission had hitherto had exclusive physical possession of the weapons); nuclear tough-mindedness became fashionable; and there was a kind of normalization of the status of nuclear weapons. The notion of nuclear weaponry as something very special was eroding.[22] To use these weapons, it was sometimes suggested, would not be all that remarkable. John Foster Dulles, the United States secretary of state from 1953 to 1959, made this position clear in a speech he gave to a ministerial meeting of the North Atlantic Treaty Organization (NATO) in April 1954. The United States, he said, believed that nuclear weapons "must now be treated as in fact having become 'conventional' … It should be our agreed policy, in case of war, to use atomic weapons as conventional weapons against the military assets of the enemy whenever and wherever it would be of advantage to do so." He chose to represent the weapons of the atomic age as "merely weapons which have greater destructive capacities" than the weapons of the past.[23] Dulles's chief, President Dwight Eisenhower, despite private misgivings, sometimes advanced similar views,[24] and during his first administration did little to resist the pro-nuclear sympathies of his senior officials. Atomic weapons, in the eyes of Washington in the mid-1950s, were integral, even ordinary, components of the free world's arsenal and would be used, "if necessary," against an enemy.

Nuclear weapons were widely seen as conferring advantage on the United States and as an expression of American leadership – leadership in science and technology and in other ways as well. "Atomic warfare should be viewed in its true light," according to Colonel George C. Reinhardt of the United States Army in 1955, "that of its harmony with American traditions – science and machines opposing brute strength. It places a premium upon military excellence, upon technical and leadership skills, rather than sheer numbers."[25] This was a common view. The Soviet Union had brawn but not, relative to the United States, brains. It relied on bulk, on quantity, on massive land forces. The United States could not and should not compete with the Soviet Union on these terms. Rather, it should emphasize quality, technique, and ingenuity. "We have the antidote" to Soviet manpower advantages, wrote Brigadier General Smith in 1955, "in our technical proficiency."[26] The United States needed to possess superior weapons and it needed to be always on the leading edge of military science. "We in the Air Force believe that air supremacy is the key to survival," asserted Jimmy Doolittle, the celebrated air commander, in 1953, "and that science is the key to air supremacy." The pursuit of superiority in weapons systems was of critical importance. "If we should have to fight," remarked Doolittle, "we should be prepared to do it from the neck up and not from the neck down."[27] Even with the challenge of a growing Soviet nuclear arsenal, the United States could still realistically aspire to strategic superiority through scientific prowess. The side which best employs nuclear weapons, argued Colonel Reinhardt, "which molds superior organization and tactics around the new tools of warfare, will possess an immense, perhaps a decisive, advantage. If there be war tomorrow, it will be a contest of skills and leadership instead of a slugging match won by attrition."[28]

Given this outlook, it was logical to conclude that United States forces must be properly prepared for such combat: combat that was expected to turn on the effectiveness with which nuclear weapons were employed. And increasingly this was taken to mean not just "strategic" bombing, but also the tactical use of nuclear weapons on land. Even as the massiveness of American attacking power was being heavily publicized in the 1950s, the tactical and allegedly more discriminating capabilities of the new military technology were being closely scrutinized, increasingly publicized, and often celebrated. The benefits of tactical nuclear weapons were highlighted in a confidential report of August 1951, which was prepared for the chairman of the Joint Congressional Committee on Atomic Energy: "Tactical atomic weapons hold forth the promise of a revolution in land war which can be compared to the revolution in air war brought about by the Hiroshima and Nagasaki bombs." Atomic weapons used tactically in a theatre of battle "are the natural armaments of numerically inferior but technologically superior nations," and their development, it was claimed, "should immeasurably strengthen Western Europe's will-to-resist, since they will decisively help to shift the balance of military power toward the free world and against the slave world."[29] The utility of nuclear weapons was not as limited as many people thought. In fact, they could be adapted to a wide range of circumstances, and they could be used in a selective manner, with due regard for local circumstances.

This was the position publicly advanced by Gordon Dean, the chairman of the Atomic Energy Commission, in a major speech in October 1951: "Because of our great technological strides, we are now entering an era when the quantities of atomic weapons available to us will be so great, and the types so varied, that we may utilize them in many different ways heretofore not possible. This means that we are gaining the capacity to meet a given situation with an atomic weapon tailored to meet that situation." He was pleased to be able to report that, "with each passing day, our design and production progress is steadily adding to the number of situations in which atomic weapons can be tactically employed against military targets."[30] There was the prospect that fire power could be packaged to provide virtually whatever degree of force was desired, small or large. A whole new spectrum of nuclear weapons was coming into being, weapons that were seen as readily usable and eminently suitable for confronting and, if necessary, defeating all sorts of concentrations of communist military force. Within a decade after Hiroshima, Washington was deeply committed to the concept of a nuclear battlefield: a battlefield in which nuclear weapons, possibly in large numbers, could be and if necessary would be used to defeat communism, whether in Asia, in Europe, or on the seas.[31]

The drift in all this thinking was to make nuclear weapons appear rather commonplace and not particularly intimidating or horrible. There was a tendency in official circles to deprecate the "public hysteria" concerning the possible employment of nuclear weapons and to deplore some of the taboos and inhibitions concerning their use.[32] These weapons, some strategists suggested, should be regarded as simply the latest phase in the evolutionary logic of weapons development. Their destructive potential, it was said, should not be treated in such an emotional manner. Nuclear weapons were here to stay; nuclear warfare could be conducted advantageously; indeed, it might actually be fought with less damage to non-combatants than the wars of the recent past. This was what Robert C. Richardson III, a brigadier general in the USAF, thought in 1960: "The development of new weapons has always been accompanied by dire predictions as to their effect on nations and civilizations. In practice the predictions never have been correct because strategies and tactics are invariably adjusted so as to derive useful returns from new weapons. The atomic development is no exception. The new tactics geared to this development actually suggest that atomic warfare in the future may be less destructive than past conventional warfare, provided we accept the use of atomic weapons as inevitable and adjust our forces and target strategy accordingly." It was both possible and desirable, he felt, to come to terms with the new weaponry and to make good military use of it. As a military man, he planned on the assumption "that there will be wars in the future, and that atomic weapons will be used to the extent that they are found to be advantageous but without necessarily resulting in more extensive destruction to the nations involved than occurred in past world wars." The field of battle could, to a considerable degree, be detached from the fabric of society, and thus civilian losses would not get out of hand. What he feared most was the failure of the United States to devise plans for the effective use of nuclear weapons and unwarranted inhibitions about using them in "small wars": "the main danger is not atomic weapons so much as ignorance or inexperience in their use."[33]

Whatever reservations there may have been about these strategic doctrines (and there were some), and despite the anxieties that were sometimes expressed, during the 1950s America embraced the bomb. Its allies, for the most part, implicitly or explicitly endorsed this embrace. Whatever doubts they had they kept mostly to themselves.

Clearly, this policy presumed a massive increase in the nuclear arsenal. If nuclear weapons were so important, numbers would really matter. Production facilities were greatly expanded, and new plants sprang up around the country. As one authority put it, this "expansion program represented one of the greatest federal construction projects in peacetime history."[34] By 1955, the Atomic Energy Commission, which was responsible for the production of nuclear materials, was the single largest consumer of electric power in the United States; its gaseous diffusion plants consumed nearly 10 per cent of the country's total electric power generation in 1956, and it had been necessary to build new power plants especially to supply that need.[35] In 1947 the United States possessed only 13 atomic bombs; in 1948 it had about 50. Thereafter the new weapons were mass produced. When Eisenhower was elected president in 1952, there were around 1,000 warheads in the American nuclear stockpile. By the time he left office in early 1961 the arsenal held more than 18,000 warheads and was still growing.[36] This was an increase of 1800 per cent in less than a decade. The few efforts to slow down or halt this extraordinary weapons build-up were completely unsuccessful. Maintaining the nuclear advantage, it was said, was crucial to the security of free people.

VARIETIES OF FEAR

There was little self-doubt in Washington (and, to a lesser extent, in the allied capitals) about this nuclearization of strategy, and this was partly a consequence of the conviction in the West that the United States nuclear arsenal existed for strictly defensive purposes. In public discourse the purpose of these forces was described as entirely (or almost entirely) retaliatory. Nuclear weapons would be used, so most people thought, only in response to aggression: in reaction to clear-cut hostile actions and to flagrant communist expansion. There was virtually no sense that these weapons might be seen by others as offensive or provocative. Nuclear weapons were, of course, threatening, but their threat was said to be part of a policy of containment: a policy which had come about as a result of communist aggression between 1945 and 1950 (Poland, Czechoslovakia, the siege of Berlin, and, finally, Korea) and which was designed to prevent further such advances by "world communism." The responsibility for the American build-up of nuclear arms, it was widely agreed, lay with the Kremlin. Moscow initiated, Washington only reacted in self-defence. If war ever were to break out, it would be because hostilities had been forced upon the West by communist aggression. The experiences of the several years after 1945 seemed to offer ample proof of the correctness of this Manichean model of world affairs.

This thinking usually explicitly denied or at least declined to acknowledge the possibility that the United States might strike first. Striking first was not the American way. An unprovoked American nuclear attack was out of the question. The United States wanted peace, and it was hardly credible that it would seek to enforce the peace through offensive action. Americans were committed to deterrence – to ensuring that war *not* erupt. As a standard reference work declared in the late 1950s: "The United States, it was generally conceded, would never try to anticipate its antagonist by striking the 'first blow'."[37]

There are several ways of scrutinizing this American self-assessment. First, it should be recognized that no other contending great power could fully accept the United States at its word. The Soviet Union, as the only such power, was *bound* to fear American nuclear might – just as the West was bound to fear Soviet military might on the ground. Even had the Kremlin been less acutely suspicious, and even had Soviet diplomacy in 1947–8 been more supple and accommodating and less belligerent – and perhaps it would have been had Stalin died in, say, 1945 instead of 1953 – the USSR would still have feared American nuclear might. This fear was an inherent consequence of the radically revised postwar distribution of power. Washington had suddenly acquired a new weapon of unprecedented destructive force, and the Soviet leadership – *any* Soviet leadership: indeed, *any* leadership of any nation that was a great power – would have inevitably feared this extraordinary American advantage. Whatever professions of peace and good will might emanate from the United States, and let us even assume that most of these professions were genuine and meant sincerely, Moscow would see, first and foremost, American power: the power to destroy, the means of lethal attack, the capacity to take the offensive. In the face of this capability, American intentions – or at least apparent intentions, declared intentions: who, after all, could ever be sure about intentions? – were not, in Soviet eyes, of primary interest. What counted most was what American state power could do abroad if it decided to act. And from Moscow's perspective, what it could do was not reassuring.

Of course, we have little knowledge of what Stalin and his associates said to one another about the atomic bomb. They were not given to public self-revelation or to keeping records for the benefit of historians. However, the little evidence we do have suggests that the Soviet leadership reacted to this revolution in weaponry as one would expect a great power in such circumstances to react: that is, with fear, with heightened anxiety, with a sense (so soon after the defeat of the German menace) of a rekindled threat to their nation's security. Several observers in Moscow during the last five months of 1945 detected signs of this fear, including officials in both the

American and the British embassies. They suspected that the birth of the atomic age under exclusive Western auspices would cause (or was, in fact, already causing) Soviet leaders to be more suspicious, more antagonistic towards the West, and more difficult to deal with.[38]

We also have the much later testimony of Nikita Khrushchev. Khrushchev was at least as inventive as most political leaders in constructing a record to make himself look wise and prudent, and his memoirs (recorded after his forced retirement in 1964) are full of those evasions, polite fictions, and kindnesses to self that are so commonplace in such reminiscences. Nonetheless, there are many passages that ring true, among them his reflections on how the Kremlin felt about the bomb in the later 1940s: "The most urgent military problem facing us after the war was the need to build nuclear weapons. We had to catch up with the Americans, who had been the first to develop atomic bombs and the first to use them in war when they dropped them on Hiroshima and Nagasaki." The fact that the United States had already used the bomb twice may well have been construed in Moscow as evidence that Washington might not be all that inhibited about using it again, against another enemy, especially if that enemy was unable to retaliate effectively. "We knew," Khrushchev continued, "that the reactionary forces of the world, led by the United States, had decided to place all their bets on nuclear weapons." This, as we have seen, was not an unreasonable inference. He then advanced a view that was more obviously a function of Soviet dogma: "We also knew that the Western imperialists were not one bit squeamish about the means they used to achieve their goal of liquidating socialism and restoring capitalism." (The imperialists, for him, were cunning and tough and would "gobble us up" if the fledgling Soviet nation were not properly vigilant.) Khrushchev portrayed Stalin in 1945 as having been "frightened to the point of cowardice," though he acknowledged, perhaps grudgingly, that "Stalin drew the correct conclusion" and, recognizing the vulnerability of the Soviet state to American attack, ordered an all-out effort to emulate the West's atomic achievement.[39]

It is not surprising that the minds of Soviet leaders turned to worst-case (or at least bad-case) scenarios. How could they *not* have imagined what a much more powerful state could do to them? Such imagining did not even require any special degree of suspiciousness – less, certainly, than that which actually afflicted Josef Stalin. Moreover, such fearful and suspicious minds were likely to take particular notice of some of the wilder voices of American anti-communism.

These were voices that spoke of preventive war: of the United States initiating a nuclear attack against the Soviet Union before it could develop its own nuclear arsenal; of the United States resolving the Cold War by turning it into a hot war while conditions were still favourable for an American victory. According to this hawkish perspective, the United States should strike while it could without fear of nuclear retaliation.

Such talk became public from time to time in the late 1940s and early 1950s[40] (see also *infra* 31–3). And while it was, in a sense, loose talk – a part of the cacophony of the American public debate – and seldom seriously considered in the White House, it is understandable that Soviet leaders would not have been as unconcerned about these muscle-flexing pronouncements as some historians think they should have been. Fear has big eyes, according to an old Russian proverb, and a nuclear-weak Moscow could not have remained unfazed by a nuclear-strong Washington that harboured prominent men who thought that a "bombs-away" strategy was the best way to deal with the evil of communism. But surely, it might be said, these men were in a distinct minority? And surely, too, everyone could see that their militant views had not been officially encouraged or endorsed? A Soviet observer, though, might have feared, not unreasonably, that their influence would grow. Perhaps their hawkish views would someday enter the American political mainstream. Who was to know? Better, surely, if you sat in the Kremlin, to expect the worst and, as much as possible, prepare for the worst. What was certainly essential from Moscow's perspective was a Soviet bomb to serve as a counterweight to the menacing American nuclear arsenal.

Few Americans acknowledged that the Soviet Union might have legitimate grounds for fearing their nation. Friendly foreigners were more inclined to see this possibility and to recognize how truculent talk in the United States about preventive nuclear war was likely to be taken seriously (maybe too seriously) in Moscow. One of these foreign observers was Sir John Slessor, who, in a lecture given at the United States Air War College in April 1948, over a year before the first Soviet atomic test, considered the possibility that Soviet fear was genuine. "I believe," he remarked, that the Russians "really are afraid they will be attacked sooner or later. It must be admitted that they are not entirely without grounds for this fear – there is some excuse for a Russian who reads the American Press imagining that it is only a question of time before the U.S.S.R. is attacked. The atom bomb was a shock to them and they are still frightened of it."[41]

Other allies of the United States sometimes expressed similar concerns about this apparent brandishing of its atomic weapons. Canada's secretary of state for external affairs, Lester B. Pearson, reported to high American officials in June 1951 that "there was a considerable body of opinion in Canada ... that the United States has come to accept the inevitability of war and is, accordingly, launched upon a program to build up strength, not to win the peace but to win the war." Significantly, the American secretary of state, Dean Acheson, in reply to Pearson, conceded: "foreign observers would find a good deal of evidence for this conclusion in our public press and radio and in the speeches of various public figures. Although such evidence exists, he said the conclusion was not true."[42]

Another approach to the proposition that Washington's nuclear posture was strictly defensive and reactive is to examine the actual implications of American nuclear doctrine as it took shape. What one finds in these doctrinal discussions, implicitly and sometimes explicitly, is a concern with being able to take the initiative and strike first. Strategists tended to speak rather vaguely about "being goaded to war," or responding to provocation, or resisting aggression; however, it was often clear from what they said that a major military objective would be (or at least should be), first, to launch United States forces before they could be caught on the ground, and second, to knock out the other side's delivery systems before they could be launched.

There was little talk in these circles of riding out a Soviet attack or of absorbing a Soviet strike before counter-attacking; and there was a recurrent vagueness about the circumstances that would justify nuclear "retaliation" by the United States. Brigadier General Smith, for example, proposed in 1955 that "once enemy intentions are clear through overt acts of aggression, retaliation is morally acceptable even before we suffer the loss of several cities."[43] This, of course, allowed much leeway for military initiative: the assessment of "intentions" and "overt acts of aggression" depends greatly on the eyes of the beholders. Easily alarmed beholders, and already hostile and deeply suspicious beholders, might have little trouble in discovering aggressive actions that would justify, in their own minds, an offensive punch for defensive purposes. In the early 1960s Melvin Laird, later President Nixon's secretary of defense, offered remarks that suggested such strategic robustness. It should be made clear to all, he said, "that the United States will take the initiative, not hesitating to strike first if the Communist Empire further moves to threaten the peace of the world, or the freedom of other peoples."

The world (especially Moscow) should know, he added, "that we reserve to ourselves the initiative to strike first when the Soviet peril point rises beyond its tolerable limit."[44] This limit he left unspecified.

Moreover, there is now strong evidence that American strategy in the 1950s included explicit designs for a nuclear first strike. While declaratory policy usually emphasized deterrence and retaliation, operational planning had in mind a more assertive posture. The Joint Chiefs of Staff stated (privately) in January 1950 that "[we] cannot accept as a premise that either the super [thermonuclear] bomb or the atomic bomb is valuable only as a weapon of retaliation."[45] Obtaining and preserving a first-strike capability was regarded by many men in the Pentagon as essential. Military officers, particularly those in the air force, were acutely conscious of the long-established advantages of striking first. And their emphasis on counterforce strategy – that is, attacks against the military assets of the enemy – was inherently pre-emptive, because it made sense only if Soviet forces could be destroyed before they left their bases. General Thomas D. White, chief of staff of the USAF, set out this argument in an address given in November 1957: "Pure air defense – the most effective air defense – is to strike the enemy forces at their home bases before they get off the ground. The next best air defense would be to attack enemy forces in the air immediately after they have been launched or as distant as possible from friendly territory. The least desirable air defense, which is really a last ditch defense, is to counter the enemy over the immediate target area."[46]

Recent historical studies are revealing the importance of these first-strike strategies. One historian has concluded, from a study of strategic thought: "The notion that the United States and not the Soviet Union would be the first nation to use nuclear weapons in the next war was not only the expectation of the SAC [Strategic Air Command] planners; it was also the principal idea upon which most of their planning was based."[47] The most careful and authoritative studies of American nuclear planning up to 1960 have been done by David Alan Rosenberg of the Naval War College, and his work leaves little doubt about the expansive way in which "deterrence" was conceived and put into practice. Waiting to be attacked, and only then counter-attacking, was not the Pentagon's idea of a satisfactory defence. As Rosenberg explains:

The priority assigned to blunting Soviet atomic capability was in effect a decision to prepare for a pre-emptive counterforce strike in the event of impending hostilities, although a strategy of counterforce and pre-emption had not been directed at the high policy level. The [Joint Chiefs of Staff] were acting simply in accordance with their understanding of their assigned responsibilities, which included, first and foremost, the defense of the nation. If pre-emptive attack prior to an enemy strike was the only means to accomplish that objective, pre-emption would be included as an option in strategic and operational plans, unless the president specifically directed otherwise. President Truman did not direct otherwise; nor, it appears, have any of his successors. [48]

Getting in the first nuclear blow thus became a central concern of strategic planners. By the end of Eisenhower's presidency, observes Rosenberg, "the Strategic Air Command had prepared and trained for nearly a decade not only for massive retaliation but also for massive preemption."[49]

A strictly retaliatory view of deterrence, then, certainly did not predominate among strategic planners during the 1950s, in part because they saw such a view as dangerously constrictive and reactive. "We don't build forces for deterrence," remarked General Nathan Twining, chairman of the Joint Chiefs of Staff from 1957 to 1960, in the mid-1960s. "We build forces for national defense – to fight. Their deterrent effect is only a peacetime by-product of their war-waging capability."[50] In the 1950s SAC's view was that it ought to have, and did in fact have, a disarming first-strike capability. This capability was thought to be of great importance in reassuring Western Europe of the firmness of the United States commitment to defend it, for this overwhelming nuclear superiority, combined with the comparative security of the United States from Soviet attack, was considered to provide a credible bulwark against Soviet expansionism. Soviet leaders, recognizing their own nuclear inferiority and realizing their vulnerability to attack, would surely refrain from overt aggression. Their fear, it was hoped, would restrain them; and this fear was thought to be at least partly a function of the first-strike capability of the United States. [51]

Perhaps the main conclusion to draw from this discussion is that, while Americans thought they had good reason to fear Soviet power (as, indeed, they and certainly their European allies had), the Soviet Union had good reason to fear American nuclear weapons. Soviet anxiety was certainly not unfounded. First-strike strategies *were* entertained in Washington; loose talk about the United States taking the nuclear initiative *was* fairly common; the potency of nuclear weapons *was* regularly celebrated; and, while Americans were confident in their own reasonableness and self-restraint, Moscow could hardly be expected to share this conviction. The Kremlin was bound to see the large and rapidly expanding American nuclear arsenal as a fearful thing, and Soviet leaders had the strongest possible incentive to respond with their own nuclear build-up, in an effort to offset this intolerable American advantage. For a few years, only the American homeland was invulnerable to nuclear devastation. Moscow, not unreasonably, was determined to level the playing field.

MORALIZING

At the height of the Cold War, in the early 1950s, the distinguished political scientist and exponent of Realism, Hans Morgenthau, pointed to a crucial dimension of United States foreign policy. He said of his government: "We have acted on the international scene, as all nations must, in power-political terms; but we have tended to conceive of our actions in non-political, moralistic terms."[52] This was not simply a matter of the United States treating its own intentions kindly, an understandable and virtually universal conceit of nation-states. Rather, it involved a persistent inclination to moralize relations of power at the expense of realistic analysis. This moralizing suffused American thinking about world politics in general and nuclear weapons in particular. Accordingly, the world was the arena for a kind of moral struggle, a contest between incompatible value systems; and nuclear weapons were seen to derive their political meaning, not so much from their intrinsic lethality as from the presumed moral purposes of their possessors.

This moralized conception of nuclear weaponry was enunciated before World War II had even ended. In a radio address of 9 August 1945, President Truman had said to his countrymen: "We must constitute ourselves trustees of this new force – to prevent its misuse, and to turn it into the channels of service to mankind. It is an awful responsibility which has come to us. We thank God that it has come to us, instead of to our enemies; and we pray that He may guide us to use it in His ways and for His purposes."[53] Such extraordinary power was, in some sense, frightening, but at least it was in good hands. As Truman put it in his Navy Day speech of 27 October 1945: "In our possession of this weapon, as in our possession of other new weapons, there is no threat to any nation ... [Our possession] of this new power of destruction we regard as a sacred trust. Because of our love of peace, the thoughtful people of the world know that that trust will not be violated, that it will be faithfully executed."[54]

These were early assertions of themes and presumptions that became commonplace in American thinking about nuclear weapons. There was the notion that the United States has both the right and the duty to act in the interests of all mankind; the view that American state power, unlike the power of other states, should not be distrusted; the idea that because American intentions were benign, its military capabilities posed no problems – except for "aggressors." Foreigners ought to understand the United States in the way that America understood itself.[55] Only "evil" powers had any grounds for fearing American strength. The possession of nuclear weapons was seen as unobjectionable when they were held by an incontestably defensive power such as the United States.

It was a nation's moral standing, then, that was crucially important. In a major speech delivered in October 1951, Gordon Dean, chairman of the Atomic Energy Commission, sought to justify his country's growing reliance on nuclear weapons and explicitly linked American world leadership, the atomic bomb, and moral virtue. He spoke of "the noble ideals of freedom and human dignity to which mankind has always aspired and which have reached their greatest fruition here in our own country." "Today," he continued, "the United States stands before the world with the lamp of liberty raised high in one hand and the atomic bomb in the other." To those who questioned this joining together of virtue and the bomb, Dean gave the following answer: "In essence, we have taken the position as a nation that war is bad, and aggression is bad, and any weapon that serves to prevent war and aggression, or to stop aggression once it has been undertaken, is good ... any other position would in all likelihood mean the end, not only of our freedom and our way of life, but of all the noble ideals to which man has aspired through the ages."[56] As Dean and many others saw it, the radical evil of communism, combined with the exceptional moral status of America, justified the central role of atomic weapons in the free world's pursuit of peace and security.

These presumptions of national righteousness were critical in the shaping of American military doctrine, with its emphasis on the vital importance of nuclear weapons, and in the rationalization of this nuclear dependence. Many Americans believed that their country enjoyed God's blessing and that they were a chosen people; they believed in the specialness of the American mission and in the essential virtue of their nation's causes. America was, as the early Puritans had held, a "Citty Upon a Hill," a satisfying image that persisted robustly into the twentieth century.[57] Its ends were noble and just; and, this being so, the means chosen to attain them were not likely to be closely scrutinized. The tools of action were less important than the moral standing of those who controlled them. The tools (that is, the weapons) commanded by a moral nation shared little in common, politically, with similar technology when commanded by an immoral nation. Political commentators, in fact, frequently resorted to the language of domestic law and order: the United States was the "policeman" confronting the "criminal elements" of the world. And policemen, of course, had to have better weapons than criminals.

American thinking about nuclear weapons in the 1950s, then, presumed a profound moral asymmetry among nations, and this highly moralized conceptualization of political relations raised some serious intellectual tensions. In its own eyes, the United States was committed to peace, freedom, and democracy. At the same time, it was championing the political value of weapons of mass destruction: weapons that were capable of unprecedented and indiscriminate slaughter and devastation; weapons that could be credibly perceived to threaten the future of civilization. The United States was pursuing "moral" ends with extraordinarily lethal means. Even if all weapons might be regarded in a certain sense as tools of terror, nuclear weapons had transformed the meaning of terror, not just for individuals but for entire societies. Yet it was just these weapons of terror that moral America chose to stress, and it partly justified this choice on the grounds of the immorality of the enemy. But this was slippery terrain. The legitimacy of Washington's security strategy depended heavily on a general acceptance of populist America's own moral self-evaluation, and Americans of enquiring mind and many foreigners were unable to swallow all of this nationalist ideological package and its sweeping political implications. The result was a persistent undercurrent of dissent, especially from the mid-1950s, both at home and abroad.

The defenders of the "great deterrent" position, faced with these challenges and striving to shore up their weaker intellectual ramparts, commonly reiterated even more forcefully their belief in the moral authority of the United States. An absolute threat from an absolute enemy tended to justify an absolute weapon. As Brigadier General Smith put it: "When an enemy is dedicated to destroy us by any means, it seems perfectly right, if not morally imperative, to utilize any conceivable weapon against him in self-defense."[58] The notion that Soviet objectives might be limited, even defensive, received no consideration in these circles. Strategic thought was formulated through concepts of totality, of all-or-nothing, of unqualified intentions. The orthodox strategists were inclined as well to draw attention to what they saw as the hypocrisy or naïveté of their anti-nuclear critics who were often described as pacifists, or proponents of appeasement, or dupes of communist propaganda. The latter charge was rooted in the fact that the Soviet Union, which was always playing nuclear catch-up and thus never had any incentive for revelling in the bomb, sponsored various "peace campaigns" during these years – campaigns that focused almost exclusively on the nuclear threat and Washington's highlighting of these weapons and conveniently overlooked the Stalinist record of military coercion, especially in eastern and central Europe. Critics of the policy of nuclear dependence found their positions linked to those of the Soviet party line, which, of course, was a tainting linkage in the eyes of Western public opinion. For the Western defenders of official wisdom, it was usually expedient to deprive the public debate of any sense of a legitimate intellectual third option: one was either pro-nuclear and patriotic or anti-nuclear and soft on communism. No other view could be taken seriously. Such political simplifiers were commonplace in a Cold War culture.

This moralizing was intimately related to national pride and national egoism. For most Americans, as for the peoples of most other states, nationalism is taken for granted. Love of country may sometimes be a source of inspiration and commendable conduct, but love can be blind and American patriotism is no exception. Of course, it was not popular in the 1950s to say so. One writer who did, the political scientist, Robert E. Osgood, declared in 1953 that "self-deception and self-righteousness reign supreme in matters of international morality, and Americans are by no means immune."[59] Such humility and realism were uncommon during these years. As I shall argue later, a price has often been paid for these nationalist self-deceptions. Policy can fail for many reasons: incompetence, impatience, lack of imagination, over-ambition, timidity, rigidity, failure of nerve. Moralism is too often omitted from such lists. It is worth recalling the admonition of the prominent American theologian, Reinhold Niebuhr, who suggested in 1953 that the United States might have more success in world affairs "if we were less sure of our purity and virtue. The pride and self-righteousness of powerful nations are a greater hazard to their success in statecraft than the machinations of their foes."[60]

JUDGMENTS

Let me conclude with four further observations.

First, while the atomic bomb was obviously a revolutionary weapon with extraordinary implications, the emphasis on air-atomic power was, in many respects, a continuation of the Anglo-American policies of strategic air power adopted during World War II. These policies had endorsed the mass bombing of civilian targets. They had rejected the distinction between combatants and non-combatants. They had sought to undermine civilian morale and the enemy's social fabric by more-or-less indiscriminate destruction from the air. The bombers' objectives were to create panic, to cause terror, to "de-house" industrial workers, and, if possible, to damage war-related industries that were located in these cities (this was commonly more an ancillary than a central goal). During 1943, 1944, and early 1945, tens of thousands of German and Japanese civilians, mostly women and children, were killed in air raids that were designed to obliterate large swaths of enemy cities (the raids on Hamburg in July 1943, Dresden in February 1945, and Tokyo in March 1945 being among the most destructive). The significance of these bombings for the eventual allied victory has been much debated and continues to be controversial, but there is no doubt about their legacy. The experience of total war between 1939 and 1945 included a tradition of saturation bombing, of wholesale destruction from the air; and this tradition was eminently compatible with the even more destructive capabilities that were revealed in August 1945 – in fact, it led logically to the strategy of air-atomic superiority that became self-conscious policy by the end of the 1940s. Postwar atomic strategy, then, very much built on what had happened immediately before.[61]

Second, American policy choices during the decade after 1945 were, perhaps, neither particularly unusual nor particularly surprising. For most Americans the atomic bomb was newfound power; and power, of course, was to be used – used to induce others to align themselves more closely with the American position, used as a persuader, used as a "tool of peace." The bomb was seen by most people, certainly from 1947 and even before, as an American advantage, an advantage that ought to be exploited (in a good sense) in the interests of national security and strengthening the United States agenda for an orderly and prosperous postwar world. There was nothing especially remarkable in these views. They were ordinary views for a great power determined to secure its immediate interests and struggling to find the means to do so in a time of radical change and turmoil.

In many respects the United States during the early atomic age was responding in a conventional manner to an extraordinary situation. And the problems it faced deserve to be sympathetically appreciated. The United States had *suddenly* become the foremost global power – it had never before had to manage such world-wide interests. The atomic bomb had *suddenly* appeared on the world scene – there were no precedents for dealing with such a powerful weapon. The colossal upheaval of 1939–45 meant that American statesmen and diplomats were bound to be scrambling to cope with radically redefined realities almost everywhere. They were often uncertain, even baffled; and they were not always able or disposed to think through the longer term implications of their actions. One of the most astute interpreters of the atomic age, Bernard Brodie, once said of the nuclear weapons policies of his country, "I see no reason to believe that any other government placed in comparable circumstances would very likely have done better."[62] Considering the political records of other great powers in this and previous centuries, and their affection for the tools of violence, it would be hard to quarrel with this judgment.

Third, American nuclear strategy can only be properly understood in relation to the Stalinist rule of its chief adversary. While Washington's eventual heavy reliance on nuclear weapons was in a sense historically logical and understandable, the acuteness of this dependency was partly a consequence of the acuteness of Stalinist repression and dogmatism, especially in eastern and parts of central Europe. The heavy hand of Stalinism, whether in Hungary or Czechoslovakia or Berlin, was hardly conducive to those habits of compromise, flexibility, and accommodation that were essential to the achievement of any sort of postwar political settlement. Stalinist rule was mostly by force, little by consent. It aroused fear and hatred and led (among most of its subjects) to sullen acquiescence. It presented a face to the outside world that was rarely attractive and often repellent. The extremities of Stalinism made the extreme American dependency on nuclear weapons easier to swallow, easier to justify. The bomb was spoken of as the absolute weapon; the Soviet Union – or "world communism" – was considered to be, more or less, an absolute evil. The argument was that the Stalinist threat, which was seen as a fundamental attack on civilized values, could be adequately met *only* by the nuclear threat (which was said by a few people at that time and has been regarded by many people since as at least an equal peril to mankind), and this was an argument that most people in the 1950s found plausible, persuasive, even self-evident. It is noteworthy that during the two years after Hiroshima, when Soviet-American relations were often difficult and strained but certainly not without hope, Washington had given little priority to its atomic arsenal, which numbered around a dozen bombs in mid-1947. It was only after 1947, when Stalin pressed for an even harsher agenda in his sphere of influence, that the United States became deeply committed, even adamantly committed, to the nuclearization of its national security policy.

Fourth, most of the crucial decisions about nuclear weapons and their development were made before 1960. The essential structure of the American nuclear presence – the arsenal of bombers, submarine-based missiles, land-based missiles, and tactical weapons – was already determined by 1960, and the changes effected afterwards, during the 1960s, 1970s and 1980s, were relatively much less important. The quantities of weapons that existed in the Reagan years were much the same as the quantities in the early 1960s. As Herbert York, a prominent military scientist of long experience, observed in 1987: "at the end of the Eisenhower administration we had plans, largely backed by solid commitments, for a strategic nuclear delivery force consisting of about 2,400 vehicles, just slightly more than we had in the mid-1980s, a quarter century later." "The remarkable thing" about the numbers of nuclear warheads, he said, and about other nuclear numbers as well, "is how much they changed during the Eisenhower administration and how little they changed since."[63] The nuclearization of American policy was a rapid, early, and precipitous development in the nuclear age. Little more than a dozen years after Hiroshima, the United States was locked into a structure of nuclear dependency that would prove to be highly resistant to future revision.

Thus, by the mid-1950s a vigorous commitment to the utility of nuclear weapons was deeply rooted in American political culture. The United States was the world's pre-eminent status quo power, and the bomb had been allotted a leading role in the preservation of the existing distribution of power. Atomic power had become a central element of America's sense of vitality, strength, and global influence. Conventional thinking was, for the most part, pro-nuclear (when it was not simply apathetic). Vested interests had quickly materialized to support and sustain this thinking: in the Pentagon, in the Atomic Energy Commission, in prominent scientific laboratories, in certain large corporations, in communities whose economies were dependent on the production of the bomb and the complex systems needed to deliver it abroad.

We can think of all this as a new establishment: a formidable network of mutually dependent interests, which included bureaucrats, congressmen, scientists, local politicians, corporate managers, academics, and workers. Once these interests were in place, they would not be easy to dislodge. They were, for the most part, products of the Cold War and would almost certainly feel threatened by any thaw in this hostile superpower relationship. For them, technical change, improved weapons systems, even an arms race of indefinite duration (to preserve or strengthen the deterrent) were desirable or at least acceptable; indeed, their technological optimism was largely unqualified. These constituencies and ideologies were at the core of the nuclear deep-freeze that the following generation lived with, a state of existence which was often at odds with the political changes and revisions of global power that were manifest during these decades. Inertia, even in the turbulent nuclear age, has been a powerful reality, especially in thought and language. The chapters that follow seek to understand both this intellectual immobility and the relationship between what people thought was happening and what was actually happening as citizens and their leaders struggled to come to terms with the remarkable political circumstances created by modern military science.

CHAPTER TWO

Standing Tall (But Naked)

With nearly everyone who came in to see me on August 7 the first topic of conversation was the atomic bomb. Everyone seemed to feel that a new epoch in the world's history had been ushered in. The scramble for the control of this new power is going to be one of the most unusual struggles the world has ever seen.

Henry A. Wallace, United States secretary of commerce,
diary entry for 7 August 1945[1]

In January 1953, as presidential power in Washington was changing hands, a study entitled "Armaments and American Policy" was submitted to the secretary of state. This report, which was prepared by a small committee of consultants chaired by J. Robert Oppenheimer, pointed to the emerging vulnerability of the United States to atomic attack and the inadequate public appreciation of this new fact of life. As these experts put it: "both the public and the responsible military authorities appear to be persuaded that the important characteristic of the atomic bomb is that it can be used against the Soviet Union; much less attention has been given to the equally important fact that atomic bombs can be used by the Soviet Union against the United States." They referred to the "unpleasant fact that the atomic bomb works both ways."[2] Moscow, they predicted, would soon have the physical capability to do to the United States what Washington could already do to the Soviet Union. The implications of this dangerous prospect were, however, poorly understood: "Official comment on atomic energy has tended to emphasize the importance of the atomic bomb as part of the American arsenal. There is an altogether insufficient emphasis upon its importance as a Soviet weapon, and upon the fact that no matter how many bombs we may be making, the

Soviet Union may fairly soon have enough to threaten the destruction of our whole society."[3]

Such recognition of the imminent vulnerability of the United States to catastrophic attack was not entirely novel in the early 1950s. There had been warnings ever since Hiroshima of the inevitable consequences of an atomic arms race: of the likelihood that the United States monopoly would not last long; of the virtual certainty that other great powers would succeed in emulating the American technological breakthrough (for they would have a powerful incentive to do so); and of the foreseeable consequence that the United States would some day – probably sooner rather than later – be vulnerable in a way that it had never been before. The writing was on the wall for those who were prepared to see it. But most were not, especially after the initial shock of August 1945 was replaced by the anxieties and alarms of the Cold War. The contest between freedom and totalitarianism had come to be seen as the world's main event; and in resolutely pursuing this contest, atomic weapons were treated as a critical advantage for the free world. It has been said that John Foster Dulles "did not fear the nuclear arms race, because he had confidence the Russians could not keep up." As the secretary of state put the matter in mid-1955: "The Soviet bloc cannot indefinitely sustain the effort to match our military output."[4] Pressing ahead on the atomic front – indeed, actually forcing the pace – was clearly the right thing to do. The Soviet Union would be no match for the United States. "Our economic base," thought Dulles, "almost equal to that of all the rest of the world together, can support indefinitely the high cost of modern weapons ... The Soviet bloc economy cannot indefinitely sustain the effort to match our military output, particularly in terms of high-priced modern weapons. Already there is evidence that the Soviet economy is feeling the strain of their present effort and that their leaders are seeking relief." The United States should "continue the pressure."[5]

Nevertheless, whatever the confidence in the atomic prowess of the United States, there was an underlying gloomy logic in this arms race that could not be entirely swept aside by patriotic boosterism. And this logic was that the initial advantage of the United States, which was rooted first in monopoly and then in massive predominance, was bound to erode; in time it might be lost altogether. In 1945–6 this logic, with its implication of future American vulnerability, had prompted considerable support for the international control of atomic energy – an extraordinary *supra*national control which, it was argued, would be in the long-term interest of United States national security. Certainly, some people believed that such control was the only way to prevent the atomic genie from running amok. This was the view of Canada's ambassador to the United States. In November 1945, Lester Pearson prepared a secret memorandum in which he spoke of the frightening prospect of a nuclearized future. If no international agreements for restraint could be reached, he predicted, "there will be competition. Such competition in the development of atomic energy for destructive purposes would be the most bitter and disastrous armament race ever run. Like every other armament race in history, it would follow the same course, of fear, suspicion, rivalry, desperation and war; only in this case the war would probably mean international suicide."[6]

By the early 1950s, however, pessimism of this sort was out of fashion. The bomb had been embraced, almost as a kind of super weapon, an arms race was well under way and gathering speed, and the United States was determined, according to some of its officials, to win this race, or at least to make good use of its nuclear superiority in resisting communist expansion. National well-being, it was widely assumed, depended on keeping clearly ahead in the race to develop advanced military technology, a goal that was considered to be eminently feasible. But this was not the whole story. Underlying the public optimism and resolve, perhaps even complacency, was anxiety: anxiety about the consequences of atomic proliferation for American security, when a presumed adversary would possess destructive powers similar to those that the United States possessed. And yet at the same time there was a reluctance to deal openly with this new and disturbing reality, partly out of the usual disinclination to deliver bad news (particularly important in American politics), partly out of fear of demoralizing the public, partly because nobody had any attractive solutions to offer. At a meeting of the National Security Council in May 1953, George Humphrey, secretary of the treasury, remarked on his own reluctance to encourage candour. He was concerned about "the wisdom of telling the American people these grim facts before we were in a position to state concretely what steps the Government would take in building a defense against atomic attack." The government should be in a position to propose a credible system of defence "at the same time that we informed them of their extreme vulnerability." The secretary of defense supported this view: because no such system was on the horizon, Charles Wilson "was far from certain that this was the right moment to acquaint the American people with the facts."[7]

During the several years before these discussions took place, a view of the Soviet Union as brutal and aggressive had become the accepted one; this understanding had certainly not changed during the early years of Eisenhower's presidency. What had changed, and continued to change, and change for the worse (from the American perspective) was the Soviet capacity to deliver atomic destruction. For most informed observers this was a sobering development, though some of them declined to admit to this anxiety in public. The proposals regarding what to do about the Soviet bomb were diverse, often ill considered, and sometimes based on fragile assumptions. However, all testified to the thinking that business as usual would not be a sufficient response. As a realistic assessment of November 1954, which had been prepared in the Department of State, put it: "The growing Soviet nuclear power and the devastating nature of total war seem certain to affect allied and u.s. attitudes toward war and risks of war."[8] War was taking on a deeper and much more troubling meaning for Americans than it ever had before (save, perhaps, at the time of the Civil War). An obvious question was posed: How should the United States respond to this expanding Soviet threat? The following discussion considers the measures that were proposed and debated, and later rejected or implemented, in the interest of United States national security, along with the state of public sentiment about the nuclear arms race, during the 1950s and 1960s.

OFFENCE/DEFENCE

The chairman of the Atomic Energy Commission, an avid backer of America's nuclear build-up, was one of a number of public figures who sounded warnings in the early 1950s about the Soviet atomic peril. "Russia has the capability today to hurt us badly," Gordon Dean wrote in January 1954, in the *Bulletin of the Atomic Scientists*, "and we are faced with the ugly fact that within two years she will have the capability to virtually destroy us if she moves first." Time was running against American security and the security of all free peoples, leading him to ask: "Can we as a nation and can the now free world permit the Soviet [Union] to reach this position of power? For reach it she will; and all the fervent hopes of free people everywhere will not deny her this terrible capability unless those hopes are reduced to action of some sort which forces open the Iron Curtain and brings a halt to her enormous weapons program."

This was strong language. Could the United States *permit* Moscow to become an atomic superpower? Perhaps the United States would have to *force open* Soviet borders and bring certain Soviet projects *to a halt*. As Dean acknowledged, he was asking "whether the free world can tolerate such power in an aggressor nation." A few lines later, to underline his concern, he asked again: "Can the nations of the now free world permit the Soviet [Union] to reach the position where if it chooses it can completely annihilate this country? Time and the unwillingness of the free world to stop the clock combine to give her this power."[9]

To stop the clock meant, of course, to act to prevent the Soviet Union from developing a formidable nuclear arsenal of its own. A great danger to the United States, as Dean and other insiders saw, was on the horizon. Perhaps it would be best to eliminate this danger at the start. The costs of not doing so and thus of allowing the danger to grow would surely be high, perhaps unacceptable, conceivably (given the Soviet lack of moral restraint) even catastrophic. Playing for time might be bad policy if time was not on one's side. For the moment the United States was strong, but even though remaining in some sense strong it also seemed to be on the verge of becoming weak. Perhaps it would be necessary to nip the evil abroad in the bud. One American writer, who had canvassed the views of members of the West German military élite in 1954, reported the common German opinion that "the strongest incentive" to preventive war on the part of the United States "was not the possession of overwhelming superiority, but rather the impending loss of American preponderance in the field of nuclear armaments and the mounting realization of the American people that they were exposed to the danger of sudden, violent death and terrible destruction."[10]

Several comments are in order regarding these responses to United States vulnerability. First, talk about preventive war (its possibility, its desirability, its feasibility) was most prevalent during the years between 1949 and 1954. These, of course, were the years when attentive Americans first became conscious of the new and disturbing state of existence that was descending upon them; and they were also the years prior to the actual realization of a Soviet operational nuclear capability – years, in other words, when the Soviet Union was still a very weak nuclear power. If there was any period when preventive war might conceivably have been feasible (and most American policy-makers never thought it was), it was during this half-decade that coincided with the peak of the Cold War.

Second, the proponents of preventive war usually held that co-existence with the Soviet Union was impossible or at least highly unlikely; that the essential character of Bolshevism ensured a more or less permanent state of global crisis; that war between West and East was probably inevitable sooner or later and, consequently, that prudent preventive action to pave the way for a better future for the free world was politically and morally defensible – and surely a lesser evil than permitting a future of communist takeovers and expansionism. While the supporters of containment held that communist expansion could be effectively resisted in the short term and that in the long term, when Moscow became more enlightened, better East-West relations could be forged, the supporters of preventive war were convinced that Soviet totalitarianism – aggressive, ruthless, barbaric – could not and never would change in the direction of moderation. They were deeply pessimistic about the politics of future superpower relations and the significance of a nuclear arsenal in Soviet hands. At the same time they were relatively optimistic about both the feasibility of a successful American nuclear first strike against Soviet military assets and the manageability of the political costs that such an extraordinary initiative would incur.

Third, the advocates of preventive war were more vocal and prominent in mainstream American politics during these years than has often been realized. The idea of preventive war was not a marginal or readily dismissed position, confined to the political fringes. Rather, its backers were to be found in Congress, in high administrative office, in the press, and especially in the United States Air Force. These were men who wanted a more positive and less reactive policy in the face of Soviet aggression. While their recommendations never came close to being implemented, the moderate popularity of their views and the attention they were given in these early Cold War debates deserve to be duly acknowledged in any reconstruction of the spectrum of reactions to the shock of vulnerability. As a result of this sense of shock, for a brief period of time the option of preventive war was debated with some seriousness and was by no means automatically ruled out of the discussible agenda for national security.[11]

After 1954, talk of preventive war largely disappeared. There was some easing of Cold War tensions (the Austrian Treaty and the Geneva summit of 1955, de-Stalinization in the Soviet Union) and talk of coexistence became more common. Although the massive retaliatory power of the United States was allotted rhetorical centre stage, strategic thinking was coming to focus more on "limited" war and on how to prevent East-West regional conflicts from degenerating into general war. But while the "solution" of preventive war had been decisively rejected, the problem of vulnerability persisted – indeed, it became more severe – and thus had to be addressed in other ways.

One of these other strategies for dealing with vulnerability highlighted the desirability of some kind of defence against enemy attack.

Gordon Dean, in his rather militant essay of January 1954, had touched on this issue: "We have still another problem of tremendous proportions; namely, that of developing measures to mitigate, in the event of an attack, the damage which would be done to this country." This means, he said, that "we had best turn serious attention to this business of civil defense and the creation of early warning devices which will permit orderly evacuation of people from target areas."[12] A potent American atomic arsenal was a necessary but not a sufficient condition of national security. Vulnerability demanded additional investments – investments in measures that could be said to be in some respect "protective."

From the early 1950s to the early 1960s there was a fairly sustained effort to interest the American public in measures designed to cope with nuclear attack. These included proposals for the dispersion of industry and population (some involving underground cities), plans for the evacuation of cities upon warning of attack, and the mass construction of bomb and fallout shelters. Contrary to the message of a book published in 1948, entitled *No Place to Hide*, the premise of civil defence planning was that it was in fact possible to hide. American society could in some meaningful way be insulated from the horrors of nuclear war. Something could be done; Americans were not helplessly exposed; prudent and sensible action could afford genuine security for American families, even in the face of nuclear aggression.

This message was insistently broadcast for over a decade. However, the results were meagre. The economic costs of civil defence were unacceptably high, the political will was wanting, the Soviet arsenal was becoming more and more potent, and the arguments of the critics of civil defence (who emphasized its futility) were forceful and persuasive. Moreover, the restrictions accepted by the superpowers in the Limited Test Ban Treaty of 1963 reduced the public anxiety about radioactive fallout and nuclear weaponry in general, and the advent of the intercontinental ballistic missile (ICBM) deprived early warning of any real meaning for civilians. Aside from a brief and farcical revival in the early Reagan years, civil defence became a dead issue. Security, so most people concluded, would have to be found by other means.[13]

A further possibility for action lay in active defence: that is, the interception and destruction of Soviet nuclear weapons before they struck their targets. During the 1950s there was much discussion about ways to detect Soviet bombers as they came down from the north and to prevent them from fulfilling their offensive missions. However, with the development of the long-range missile and, in the 1960s, the deployment of a large arsenal of Soviet missiles, both on land and in submarines, these plans to deal with bombers were rendered obsolete and largely irrelevant. Strategists and military scientists then turned their attention to the prospect that systems could be devised to shoot down Soviet missiles before they could hit the United States, which was an even more daunting task than the interception of bombers. These proposals, for anti-missile missiles, culminated in the great Anti-Ballistic Missile (ABM) debate of the late 1960s and early 1970s. This debate pitted advocates of supposedly defensive weapons, weapons intended to protect either American weapons or American citizens (both types of protection were at issue), against sceptics who argued that the protection of citizens was impossible, that no defensive system could cope with a determined nuclear attack (at least one city-busting multi-megaton warhead would always get through), and that deploying defences would simply force the other side to crank up its nuclear offences in order to be assured of overwhelming any such defences. The sceptics won both the intellectual and the political battle, and the result was the ABM Treaty of 1972. In accepting limits on ABM systems, both superpowers resigned themselves to what they had regretfully concluded they simply could not change – that is, a state of mutual vulnerability.[14]

INSECURITIES

For Americans, vulnerability crept up on them, by fits and starts, during the 1950s and 1960s. There were moments of alarm and panic, followed by phases of relative quiescence and apparent serenity. Sometimes there was no clear connection between the degree of the public's concern about vulnerability and the actual facts of Soviet power. Worry was subjective; it was rooted in perceptions, which might or might not be connected at a given moment to actual Soviet capabilities. And worry could be and sometimes was alleviated by government actions that were little more than symbolic gestures, albeit comforting ones. People might be reassured, at least for a while, even as their actual exposure to danger remained unchanged or increased. There were also time-lags in knowledge: lags between the understanding of those with inside knowledge and the understanding (or lack thereof) of a broader public which was often kept deliberately ill informed about the disturbing realities of the accelerating arms race.

The discrepancy between the public and the expert awareness of vulnerability was particularly pronounced in the mid-1950s. Many concerned scientists and government officials already had a good idea of what was happening, politically, in the modern age of mass-produced multi-megaton weapons and what in the future was possible or imminent. The future, they could see, was one in which a handful of Soviet or American bombs could pack as much explosive punch as all the firepower used by all the combatants in all of World War II. The implications for the United States of America of this new state of existence were startling, and because they were startling they were not easy to confront.

The public was first and foremost in search of reassurance, of some sense that apparently disturbing developments were being well managed and were therefore, perhaps, not so disturbing after all. This accounts in part for the popularity of President Eisenhower's Atoms for Peace speech to the United Nations in December 1953, which focused political attention on the prospect of atomic energy for civilian purposes. It was a great public relations success and cheered a lot of people up, but changed little if anything with regard to United States security and insecurity. People were eager for messages of hope; they wanted to feel that they could draw on their successes of the past to face successfully the present and the future. They wanted to be able to play from strength, to be true to their own native American traditions; hence their faith in the efficacy of their own powers of practical and technological creativity. Americans were inclined to have confidence in the value of nuclear weapons, despite their country's growing vulnerability to nuclear attack, wrote the editor of the *Bulletin of the Atomic Scientists* in October 1953: "the American tradition is to trust, in war as well as in peace, in the superior American capacity for rapid development of new technological methods and devices. Most Americans believe that in a race of technological weapons with any other nation, America is bound to make the better showing and that therefore we have no reason to be afraid of such a race – a proposition in which, unfortunately, only the first half is correct."[15]

The implications of a Soviet nuclear arsenal were not pleasant to contemplate, and it is hardly surprising that many Americans in the 1950s – probably most Americans – preferred not to dwell on these gloomy realities. People took comfort in such notions as "peace through strength"; they were reassured by the well publicized and imposing posture of the Strategic Air Command and its long-range bombers, which were much celebrated in the popular media (as in the 1955 Hollywood movie, *Strategic Air Command*, starring James Stewart). People had confidence in American science and technology. They preferred to think in terms of historical continuities rather than of the acute rupture in world affairs that some of the nuclear scientists so often spoke about. The erosion of American security, and the loss of America's exceptional status as an invulnerable nation, were painful to ponder and thus often put out of mind. Americans liked to be confident and think positively, and their government was reluctant to challenge this sunny optimism with too many disturbing facts. Anyway, it always seemed in Washington that there was enough to do in contending, firmly and resolutely, with the exigencies and emergencies of the moment.

This mood of moderate contentment was abruptly challenged in October 1957, when the Soviet Union, which had been widely regarded as a rather backward society, put the world's first satellite into orbit. The launching of Sputnik was a disturbing event, especially to the American public who were not accustomed to their nation being anything but Number One. American technological superiority had been largely taken for granted; in fact, it was assumed to be one of the pillars, along with free enterprise, of the nation's security. Suddenly these assumptions were called into question. Sputnik was a dramatic leap forward in science and the Russians had done it first. James Killian, who was appointed the first presidential adviser for science and technology shortly after Sputnik and was certainly a well-informed public figure, recalled in his memoirs how "the news of *Sputnik* found me – and most of the nation – psychologically vulnerable and technically surprised." "What I felt most keenly," he remembered, "was the affront to my national pride." This was a common reaction. Moscow's technological feat, in a field of importance to America, "did violence," as Killian put it, "to a belief so fundamental that it was almost heresy to question it: a belief I shared that the United States was so far advanced in its technological capacity that it had in fact no serious rival. That others possessed their share of technology I was certainly aware, but somehow I pictured them all laboring far behind this country, looking toward the United States for guidance, envying us our skills, our trained capacity, and above all our enormous industrial substructure that could be put to the task of converting advanced technological notions into performing hardware. Now this faith was shaken by *Sputnik*."[16]

Of course, Sputnik threatened more than just pride. It was also a sign that the next phase of the arms race might be won not by the United States but by the Soviet Union. The British ambassador in Washington certainly shared this concern, and in a despatch to the foreign secretary in early 1958 he summarized the conclusions of a new American study on "International Security: The Military Aspect," which were that "unless immediate steps are taken, there may be as little as two years before the point is reached at which the balance of strategic power begins to shift in favour of the Soviet bloc in a trend which might be irreversible in any foreseeable future."[17] Sputnik heralded, in the public mind and to a degree in reality, the beginning of the missile age, for powerful rockets were required to put satellites into orbit. These rockets were potential bearers of nuclear warheads, delivered over distances of thousands of miles. They would be able to travel from the Soviet Union to the United States in 25 to 30 minutes. They would be able to strike their targets virtually without warning. Some people worried that they would make bombers, of which the United States had hundreds, largely obsolete. Clearly, ballistic missiles were potent new weapons. And, in the minds of many Americans in the later 1950s, the Soviet Union was ahead – dangerously ahead – in the missile race.

There arose, then, a new and more focused sense of vulnerability, the "missile gap." This perceived threat was prominent in public debate for some three years, from shortly after Sputnik until John F. Kennedy became president in 1961. Alarm bells were rung loudly and often. It was predicted that the Soviet Union would soon be deploying dozens and then hundreds of long-range missiles and that the United States would be left perilously behind in this competition. Soviet superiority in missiles came to be taken for granted by most people, including many reputed experts. In a book published in 1961, Henry Kissinger, long before he left Harvard to become national security adviser to Richard Nixon, accepted the missile gap as a virtual certainty and Soviet missile superiority as beyond doubt.[18] This was a time when public anxiety about American vulnerability was overt and pervasive. The sense of danger, immediate or imminent, was markedly higher than in previous years. Strategists were especially concerned about the vulnerability of American bases, notably air force bases at home and abroad, for it was argued that a few dozen well-placed Soviet missiles could destroy most of SAC's bombers on the ground and thus deprive the nation of the mainstay of its security, that is, its capacity for nuclear retaliation against any attack. These worst-case scenarios seemed plausible to many people, as was indicated by the favourable prominence attained by an article published by Albert Wohlstetter in early 1959, entitled "The Delicate Balance of Terror." He suggested that Moscow, with its arsenal of ballistic missiles in place, might no longer be deterred by an America that was both undefended and, conceivably, newly vulnerable to a disarming Soviet nuclear first strike. Perhaps the supposed balance of terror was about to become an imbalance, with the United States, as various observers imagined, the only justifiably fearful power.[19]

The missile gap was entirely unfounded. Rarely, perhaps, have predictions about future power relations been so completely off-base. The missile gap was a phantom, as had been the bomber gap of the mid-1950s (when Soviet bomber capabilities were grossly over-estimated). What actually materialized in the early 1960s was a re-verse missile gap: that is, a pronounced American advantage in the number of long-range missiles, based on land and in submarines. The scale of the strategic balance never favoured Moscow during the missile gap scare; and during Kennedy's presidency the contin-ued preponderance of American nuclear striking power was openly acknowledged and evident to all, including the men in the Kremlin. Indeed, it is probable that Premier Khrushchev's recognition of his country's nuclear inferiority, and the failures of Soviet missile de-velopments relative to those in the United States, contributed to his rash decision to try to mitigate the imbalance by placing medium-range missiles in Cuba in 1962.[20] This was a time when the USSR had only a handful of long-range missiles (probably no more than 20 ICBMS), while the United States had several hundred missiles able to reach the Soviet Union as well as its formidable bomber force.

By the early 1960s some American officials believed that their country possessed a war-winning nuclear capability, which they considered both a good thing and a vital advantage that could be maintained for some time. True, the United States was vulnerable to considerable destruction and this was clearly regarded as a prob-lem. However, the much more severe vulnerability of the enemy was psychologically reassuring and a source of robust self-confi-dence in the Pentagon, where the ability to fight and win all sorts of wars, not just to deter them, remained a top priority. Certainly, much of Washington's official rhetoric concerning nuclear weapons during the Kennedy administration and the early Johnson years was notably hawkish, even smug: it was the talk of men who knew and took satisfaction in the fact that their nation was (in terms of nuclear numbers) well ahead. The conventional wisdom of late 1962 was well summarized by one knowledgeable strategist, Morton Halperin. "Should a war occur," he wrote,

the United States could probably expect to win, although the amount of damage that it would suffer in such a war has steadily been increasing. Sometime in the late 1950s the American strategic position vis-à-vis the Soviet Union switched from that of total predominance to relative superi-ority. Prior to this time, although the Soviets could perhaps have made significant gains in local areas including Western Europe, they could not have inflicted any damage of significance on the United States. At the present time while the United States still apparently has strategic superiority, the Soviets might be able to inflict major damage on the United States even in the event of an American first strike. At present we are in a period in which there remains a premium on striking first and in which there continues to be an American predominance of strategic forces such that the United States is likely to win any central war.[21]

Around the time of the Cuban missile crisis, the Soviet Union had a strong incentive to avoid conflict escalation. If there were ever any temptations to strike first, pre-emptively, these temptations were much more likely to be felt in Washington than in Moscow.

It was only from the mid-1960s that the Soviet build-up of long-range nuclear striking power became incontestably massive. As the post-Khrushchev leadership gave firm backing to the agenda of the Soviet military, the USSR deployed missiles at a remarkable rate. In contrast to the late 1950s, when the United States seriously over-estimated the Soviet expansion of nuclear arms, in the mid-1960s Washington underestimated the Kremlin's determination to seek a kind of nuclear parity. Suggestions that Moscow would probably settle for a smaller force than that of the United States were soon disproven, and by the beginning of the 1970s the Soviet Union had about 1600 long-range missiles, almost as many as the United States then possessed. Each side seemed to possess a survivable nuclear capability; neither side could reasonably fear that its own arsenal would be wiped out by a surprise attack from the other; and neither could reasonably conceive of striking first itself without being obliterated in return.

A state of mutual deterrence had been postulated by some strategists for several years. In the mid-1950s, for example, a German military officer had "considered it quite conceivable that the United States and the Soviet Union might eventually attain some kind of thermonuclear balance, 'a state of mutual deterrence which might help buttress peace, just as the two pillars of a Gothic arch support a tremendous weight'."[22] To some degree, however, the announcements of the arrival of mutual deterrence had been premature. For at that time the United States had been only partly deterred by the existence of nuclear weapons; and certainly the Kremlin had not felt that deterrence was mutual. A full mutuality of deterrence was only recognized by both major players from around the late 1960s. It was only then that strategic thought and the actual balance of destructive power came into reasonable alignment. Even though mutual deterrence had been on the horizon for a number of years, it did not seem to most people in both East and West to be a compelling political reality until almost twenty-five years into the nuclear age.

By the late 1960s, then, certain basic facts about the nuclear age appear to have been widely accepted. Destruction was easy and potentially unlimited, but any nuclear attack was likely to be suicidal. The task of attacking was so much easier than the task of defending that there was really (in contrast to all times in the past) no contest between the two. Even a great power could not ultimately defend itself. It could only deter a more or less equally potent adversary from striking first. The capacity to retaliate with a devastating blow came to be acknowledged as the basis for what was still called, rather inappropriately, security. In fact, both sides were inescapably insecure because both were physically unprotected. The Soviet Union had been living with this vulnerability since 1945, and living with it fearfully for most of those years. For the United States, real vulnerability was, objectively, a more recent development, though its severity had grown steadily during the 1950s and 1960s.

Neither side was pleased with the stalemate that had emerged. However, the United States was the more evidently frustrated and discontented. Americans, after all, had until very recently been an especially favoured people – chosen, so many of them thought – and relatively insulated from the nastiness of foreign powers and threats from abroad. Moreover, for some two decades the United States had emphasized the value of nuclear superiority; and its leaders, much more than those in Moscow, had touted the political utility of nuclear weapons. Consequently, the erosion and later effective elimination of nuclear superiority could hardly have been expected to sit well psychologically with either American leaders or the American public. The United States had experienced a descent from strength to relative weakness; or, to put the matter differently, it had been obliged to settle for a tie in a rivalry in which it had initially predominated. In contrast, a parity in vulnerability was something of a gain for the Kremlin, given the pronounced nuclear imbalance of earlier years. Thus, while the Soviet Union entered the 1970s with some cause for satisfaction, Americans were more likely to feel dissatisfied, or let down, or even in some sense cheated, and these feelings were very much reinforced by the débâcle of Vietnam. The United States, during these years of a perceived change in the correlation of forces (alleged or real American losses and alleged or real Soviet gains), became less smug and more agitated, while the Soviet Union under Leonid Brezhnev became more smug and dogmatic and often arrogant in its diplomacy. In these revised psychological circumstances, any political understanding that could be forged between the two capitals was bound to be tenuous and easily torn apart. The unpleasant consequences of these poisoned relations became especially transparent in the early 1980s.

WHAT IS STRENGTH?

While many attentive Americans had resigned themselves by the late 1960s to a world of mutual deterrence, which inescapably meant a vulnerable America, the ideological right found this state of existence unacceptable, even intolerable. These people could stomach neither parity nor "nuclear sufficiency." What was important to them was superiority; and in their view nuclear superiority was both crucial for United States security and attainable in practice. They objected vigorously to the erosion of America's nuclear superiority – an erosion that they regarded as fundamentally voluntary, as in some sense freely chosen by rather than forced upon their government. Thus they would speak of Washington's "unilateral abandonment" of nuclear superiority. Given the necessary political will, they argued that it was possible to stay ahead in the race for military-technological predominance. This was the view of Senator Barry Goldwater and his many supporters in the 1960s, including Ronald Reagan. As one military writer asserted in 1967, in words that would have been generally endorsed on the political right: "Strategic superiority has been the ultimate support of u.s. foreign policy in the last decade. For the near future, it is the ultimate guarantee of our own and the Free World's security and the best insurance against nuclear war. Conversely, u.s. failure to maintain superiority would be the strongest possible inducement for the Communists to accelerate aggression at whatever level of conflict seems to them most advantageous."[23]

According to this school of thought, deterrence was not a fact of life but rather a false doctrine. It stifled American initiative; it unjustly and unwisely constrained the American military; and it left America at the mercy of foreigners. Nathan Twining, a former chairman of the Joint Chiefs of Staff (1957–60), argued this case in a book published in 1966, *Neither Liberty nor Safety*. The "assumption" of mutual deterrence, he complained, "places the population and the industrial base of the United States and the Free World in a condition of perpetual hostage to the u.s.s.r. ... we, as free people, can no longer control our own destiny; the national survival depends upon the will and judgment of an enemy."[24] This was, if not an abomination, certainly very hard to swallow. Other voices on the right, retired officers and civilians, expressed similar frustrations with what they saw as misguided government policy. Settling for mutual deterrence was in their view unnecessary, unacceptable, and defeatist. American military superiority, which rested in nuclear superiority, was essential for world peace, and to preserve this dominance the United States must continue to keep ahead in the arms race through ever more technological breakthroughs. Two years before he became the Republican party's nominee for president, Goldwater championed these views in a book entitled *Why Not Victory?*: "I do not subscribe to the theory that nuclear weapons have changed everything ... We have in the nuclear bomb an advance in weaponry, and terrible though that advance is, it still is merely a more efficient means of destruction. In a historical and relative sense, it can be compared with the advance made in military operations by the invention and adaptation of gunpowder to war-making and the development of aerial warfare and strategic bombing missions."[25]

By the end of the 1960s, however, these traditionalists were in something of a quandary. They had advocated that the United States pursue the technological armaments race resolutely and with vigour; and they had argued in favour of preserving what they called strategic superiority. However, this superiority had largely slipped away; some critics were even claiming that the idea of nuclear superiority was meaningless. The traditionalist view of power saw little ambiguity in it; strength, according to this thinking, could in principle be assessed in the customary manner, which highlighted the importance of lethal firepower and the ability to deliver it. However, it was becoming increasingly evident to others that nuclear destructiveness was a peculiar sort of strength, for it was not at all clear that this strength could be used to achieve desirable political goals. Each of the two major contestants had and would retain the capacity under all conceivable circumstances to obliterate the other. How, then, could this power to destroy be translated into political influence if the potential destroyer (or nuclear coercer) would inevitably face retribution? These were not conditions that were easily assimilated by traditional strategic minds.

It is noteworthy that some of the basic dilemmas of military strategy in the nuclear age had been apprehended, sometimes clearly, sometimes uncertainly, soon after Hiroshima. An interesting expression of a somewhat reluctant and partial acknowledgment of revolutionary change is found in a work published just after World War II by a British admiral, Sir Gerald Dickens. Dickens was confronting the question of what impact the bomb was likely to have on naval power: "It may be that some day the atomic weapon will add very largely to the power of navies. A nation having command at sea might be able to threaten a land power from an almost infinite number of directions. We have not seen the last of the battleship and perhaps she will one day appear with a battery of guns firing atomic missiles at ranges of a thousand miles or more." These were the words of a man who was concerned first and foremost to ensure that naval power remain vibrant and strategically relevant. But he went on to touch on a potential snag in this optimistic future: the pointlessness of such warfare. "While we hope that war of such an insane pattern will never be fought we can at least hope that if it did [occur] we should be able to extract a mighty retribution before we went under – with everyone else." Dickens appears to have been a fatalist, for wars, he assumed, were integral to the human condition: "Wars came to us with Original Sin. When we sin no more as individuals no one, presumably, will want to make war. As things are, all we can do is, by moral and physical means together, to lessen the chances of war and, when it comes, to soften its impact to the world in general wherever this is possible."[26]

Another admiral, an American, William Leahy, who had been a member of the Joint Chiefs of Staff and later chief of staff to Presidents Roosevelt and Truman, had similarly mixed feelings about the bomb and the future of warfare. In the conclusion to his memoirs, published in 1950, Leahy regretted the totality of modern war. "The lethal possibilities of atomic warfare in the future are frightening," he wrote. "Employment of the atomic bomb in war will take us back in cruelty toward non-combatants to the days of Genghis Khan ... These new and terrible instruments of uncivilized warfare represent a modern type of barbarism not worthy of Christian man." Of course, the United States had already used the bomb in warfare, and Leahy acknowledged "a practical certainty that potential enemies will develop it in the future and that atomic bombs will some time be used against us." Here was an assessment that was clear-headed and pessimistic, and sensitive to the long-standing ideal, often not realized in practice, of humanity in warfare. He was certainly offering no welcome for the latest breakthrough in military science. However, in his final words he almost completely reversed direction and recorded a grudging endorsement of the air-atomic orthodoxy that was then (the late 1940s) taking shape: "I am forced to a reluctant conclusion that, for the security of my own country ... there is but one course open to us: Until the United Nations, or some world organization, can guarantee ... that the world will be spared the terrors of atomic warfare, the United States must have more and better bombs than any potential enemy."[27]

The reflections of these two admirals testify to the ambivalence and confusion that have been characteristic of thinking about nuclear weapons ever since their birth. Nuclear warefare was expected to be, in the words of these military men, "insane," "frightening," and "uncivilized." They and others at the time were wondering if the social fabric could survive such combat; they feared that war of such destructiveness might not be war at all but rather an all-devouring catastrophe, unjustified by any rational objective. At the same time, however, they could not really imagine that the institution of war could be or would be abolished. And if wars could and probably would be fought, one might hope but should not expect that sovereign states would hold back from using potentially their most decisive weapons, especially if their backs were to the wall. There was a sense, on the one hand, among these strategists that the international control of nuclear weapons was desirable, even necessary. But, on the other hand, because (it was widely thought) such control was probably not then feasible, perhaps it was best to act prudently and traditionally; to "maintain the peace" through superior strength, which was taken to mean nuclear strength, and to hope that at some time down the road, circumstances might make it possible to try again to manage in a less competitive manner the perils of what a prominent book of 1946 had called *The Absolute Weapon*.

A weapon that was or might be absolute had a peculiar bearing on the question of state security, which sovereign nations consider to be their raison d'être. In the 1947–8 volume of *The United States in World Affairs*, the series published annually by the Council on Foreign Relations, John Campbell included a discussion of postwar security and the relationship between the military and the non-military instruments for achieving security. "Few officials," he thought, "military or civilian, would agree that success in the quest for security depended in the long run on armed forces and military measures rather than on political and economic policies aimed at world stability and world progress. The United States possessed, already, the atomic bomb. It gave us an unchallengeable military position but had brought security neither to the American people nor to the world."[28] Here was a clear recognition of the limitations of any heavy reliance on nuclear weapons. However, such sentiments, which were fairly widespread in 1946 and 1947, became less common in 1948 and after: the exigencies of the intensifying Cold War – Czechoslovakia, Berlin, China, Korea, fears of espionage and subversion – made rearmament and military preparedness seem appropriate and acceptable. As the hopes for a political settlement and for collective security withered, the grounds for questioning the utility of military force, particularly nuclear force, were increasingly pooh-poohed or simply ignored.

Of course, the change in convictions that led to support for a nuclear build-up had no power to prevent what was bound to happen – that is, the increasing vulnerability of the United States – though these convictions undoubtedly helped many people to sleep at night and diverted their minds from grim realities. In time, however, a clearer understanding emerged, at least in some circles. This deeper understanding focused on a radical development: a fundamental transformation in the nature of power. Power no longer meant what people had traditionally thought it had meant. The relevance of military force to political purpose had lost clarity and persuasiveness. An academic work of 1959 offered a lucid formulation of these new terms of political existence:

Even the most highly organized and most strongly armed country or group of countries can now be destroyed without the necessity of first breaking the traditional "hard shell" of surrounding defense ... *Permeability* presages the end of the traditional protective function of state power and territorial sovereignty. The chief external function of the modern state therefore seems to have vanished. Utmost power in the possession of one state goes hand in hand with utmost impotence to counter the like power that others have.

What statesmen and societies confronted, in short, was the coexistence of "extreme power together with utmost vulnerability."[29]

Some years later, Henry Kissinger, while reflecting on the state of world politics in the late 1960s, made a similar point about the new nature of power. "Until the beginning of the nuclear age it would have been inconceivable that a country could possess too much military strength for effective political use; every addition of power was – at least theoretically – politically useful. The nuclear age destroyed this traditional measure. A country might be strong enough to destroy an adversary and yet no longer able to protect its own population against attack. By an irony of history a gargantuan increase in power had eroded the relationship of power to policy."[30] People had come to speak without hesitation of "the superpowers"; and yet these were very odd superpowers for both of them stood tall and were naked simultaneously. This was a most peculiar duality. Much energy was expended by both governments in trying to conceal the fact of nakedness while loudly proclaiming the fact of lethal capability.

Being able to destroy was one thing; being able to influence the will of another people was a different matter. And yet it had come to be widely assumed in the 1950s that a large nuclear arsenal was a valuable source of such influence. It afforded "the community of free nations," according to John Foster Dulles in May 1952, "vast new possibilities of organizing a community power to stop open aggression before it starts and reduce, to the vanishing point, the risk of general war." The new weapons were relevant not only to the military for "in the hands of the statesmen, they could serve as effective political weapons in defense of peace."[31] This orthodoxy had its critics, one of the most prominent of whom was George Kennan, the writer, diplomat, and originator of the policy of containment in 1946–7. Kennan set out his objections to this over-re-liance on nuclear weapons in his 1957 Reith Lectures on the BBC:

the weapon of mass destruction is a sterile and hopeless weapon ... which cannot in any way serve the purposes of a constructive and hopeful foreign policy ... The suicidal nature of this weapon renders it unsuitable both as a sanction of diplomacy and as the basis of an alliance ... There can be no coherent relations between such a weapon and the normal objects of national policy. A defence posture built around a weapon suicidal in its implications can serve in the long run only to paralyze national policy, to undermine alliances, and to drive everyone deeper and deeper into the hopeless ex-ertions of the weapons race.[32]

A generation later, in 1983, Kennan found no reason to revise his basic position. One "of our great postwar mistakes," he said, "had to do with our embracing the nuclear weapon as the mainstay of our military posture, and the faith we placed in it to assure our military and political ascendancy in this postwar era ... by this com-mitment to a weapon that was both suicidal and unsuitable to any rational military purpose we incurred, in my opinion, a heavy share of the blame for leading large parts of the international community into the most dangerous and fateful weapons race the world has ever known."[33] What had been pessimistically imagined in 1945–6 – by Lester Pearson, by the physicist Niels Bohr and some of his colleagues, and by many others – seemed to Kennan to have become a political reality by the early 1980s. The world, according to this perspective, was exceptionally dangerous, fractured, and mil-itarized. Moreover, the superpowers faced the impotence of their own destructive power. The power to devastate was undeniable, but the utility of this power had become ever more elusive, questionable, and problematic. The revolutionary power of science had raised doubts about the traditional assumptions of state sovereignty, notably the ultimate ability of the sovereign state to wage war rationally in the service of its political interests.

NUCLEAR PEACE

The scepticism of Kennan and others who had reached similar conclusions was accorded only limited approval by both main street America and experts in strategy. For there was a conventional response to this view, whether the view was offered by Kennan and like-minded intellectuals or by peace activitists and critics of United States policy, and this was the assertion that *nuclear weapons have kept the peace*. These words, or slightly different words bearing the same message, were uttered and printed millions of times. They became staple intellectual fare in the later twentieth century. The claim they made was at the heart of thinking about nuclear deterrence or, more accurately, about the nuclear threat, which was widely regarded as the foundation of the West's policies for security and defence. In 1955, when William Attwood, a journalist, visited the weapons laboratory at Los Alamos, New Mexico, the eight scientists he spoke with one evening expressed what was already a commonplace opinion. None of them, he recalled, "admitted to having any misgivings about producing weapons that would conceivably destroy civilization and even life on our planet. They were convinced that America's stockpile of atomic bombs had been the biggest factor in preventing Soviet aggression so far and that continuing research was the best insurance against aggression in the future."[34]

Here was the central rationale of America's leading role in the nuclear arms race – a rationale that soon took on a life of its own. Disarmament, perhaps, was a worthy ideal and ought not to be put out of mind. But in the real world of Soviet power and intense hostility it was essential for America, as the traditional metaphor would have it, to keep its powder dry. Until some satisfactory political settlement could be achieved, "we have literally no choice," as a document circulated by the National Planning Association in 1954 asserted, "but to continue our preparations for the grim eventuality of thermonuclear warfare and to carry on the cold war at whatever costs on all fronts."[35] The Soviet Union was widely seen as a consciously aggressive power, probably with limitless ambitions; and there was a consensus that the only way to deal with such a threat to peace was through a kind of benign terror, that is, restraint through fear. Accordingly, weapons of mass destruction were to be actually welcomed. And as the editor of the *Bulletin of the Atomic Scientists* remarked in 1956: "If one has to rely on terror weapons to keep peace, then obviously, the worse the terror, the better the chances of peace."[36]

This became a common refrain (though usually less bluntly expressed) in the 1950s and persisted as a piece of conventional wisdom for years thereafter. National strength was closely identified with nuclear "strength" – the capacity for virtually unlimited destruction. This extraordinary nuclear threat would intimidate would-be aggressors; and if war should unhappily break out, nuclear weapons, especially battlefield weapons, would (it was hoped) permit the free world to achieve some sort of political victory. "Deterrence" was frequently appealed to as the reason for strategic policy decisions and for the "modernization" of weapons systems. Indeed, almost every technical innovation in nuclear weaponry and every new operational capability was recommended on the grounds that it would "enhance our deterrent" and thus serve the cause of peace. (This thinking is discussed at greater length in chapter 4.)

Doubts were soon raised about this emerging orthodoxy, sometimes pointedly and vigorously, sometimes discreetly and cautiously. The doubters pointed to several causes for concern. One was the impact of the nuclear threat on the other side – an impact that might not be exactly what the deterrer wanted it to be. The psychology of nuclear deterrence, it was suggested, might well be more complicated than was commonly realized. Bernard Brodie had some sensible things to say about this matter in his *Strategy in the Missile Age* (1959). Deterrence, he observed, "depends on a subjective feeling which we are trying to create in the opponent's mind, a feeling compounded of respect and fear, and we have to ask ourselves whether it is not possible to overshoot the mark. It is possible to make him fear us too much, especially if what we make him fear is our over-readiness to react, whether or not he translates it into clear evidence of our aggressive intent." Here was an astute acknowledgment of the hazards of the robust nuclear posture of the United States: the danger that this posture might be perceived abroad as provocative, as arrogantly threatening; and that, if so perceived, an alarmed adversary might react in a manner that served no one's interest. "We know from history," Brodie observed, "that nations have sometimes taken measures for their security which produced negative results, that is, which precipitated an unwanted and perhaps disastrous war."[37] Intense fear was not the best guarantee of prudent and judicious action; indeed, it was one likely cause of events getting out of hand and of war coming about less from deliberation than from blundering and inadvertence.

A system of deterrence, rooted in mutual menace, in mutual terror, might be in some sense stabilizing, at least in the short term. But what about the long haul? Could peace through such terror be expected to last indefinitely? Even some of those who supported Washington's pursuit of nuclear superiority argued that other things had to be done as well, beyond simply preparing for atomic war. "Sooner or later," remarked John J. McCloy, an influential member of America's foreign policy élite, in 1956, "some alternative to the race for armaments will have to be found. United States policy planning should devote utmost energy to devising such a break-through. Our willingness to call off the armaments race if a bona-fide plan for control and reduction can be found should constantly be emphasized, and our search ... for such plans as are likely to be considered by the Soviet Union should be at least as vigorous as our development of [atomic] strength." Along with some others McCloy had a sense of the danger, should national security policy become indissolubly wedded to deterrence and the possibilities for a political settlement foreclosed: "Breaking the atomic deadlock ought to be a major policy objective. The initiative we can develop lies in the field of peace rather than in preparation for war."[38]

According to one political outlook, the balance of nuclear terror afforded a solid basis for security; but from another perspective, this relationship of mutual fear represented merely a postponement of the catastrophe that would always be waiting to happen. The nuclear threat could not be expected to work forever – that is, to remain always unfulfilled. As a sceptical British writer, G.F. Hudson, observed in the mid-1960s: "It is all very well to talk of 'living with the bomb', but mankind cannot live with the bomb. As long as the great nuclear armouries exist, they are part of the system of international power politics. If they are not dismantled in time, the day will come when the game of threat and counterthreat will be played once too often."[39] A day of reckoning could be put off only for so long, but for long enough, everyone must hope, to allow statesmen and their advisers to devise other strategies for the long-term survival of imperilled civilization. The time bought through deterrence should be put to creative use. "Atomic deadlock," thought the editor of the *Bulletin of the Atomic Scientists* in 1956, "can have positive value only if man uses the breathing spell it provides, to develop a permanent foundation for peace without terror."[40]

In reviewing the debate and comment on nuclear weapons during roughly the first fifteen years after Hiroshima, one cannot help but notice the considerable fancy intellectual footwork that emanated from the political establishment and its supporters. First, the exclusive American possession of atomic weapons was said to be vital to the free world's postwar security. Then, when this monopoly was suddenly terminated, it was said that security depended on preserving an overwhelming American nuclear superiority and the capacity to use it unilaterally. And, finally, when this superiority was eroding and the United States was becoming vulnerable to attack, it was said that security depended on mutual deterrence and maintaining a balance of awesome power, which would make war unthinkable. This was all part of the process whereby Americans and their allies adjusted to what they were unable to change and tried to make the best intellectually of what had actually and disagreeably occurred: that is, the creation of a condition of universal defencelessness. Throughout these years a lot of intellectual energy was invested in demonstrating that the policies adopted by Western capitals to ensure their citizens greater security were all for the best, even as ever more destructive enemy force was targeted against them. As one writer, Coral Bell, remarked in 1957: "There is a certain irony in the reflection that, after it had been proclaimed as an official item of faith for years that peace was preserved by the western monopoly of, or western superiority in, air-atomic power, the major reaction to the loss of any such decisive superiority (the hard reality of the atomic stalemate) was a general conviction that the new situation was a still better preservative of peace."[41]

Perhaps this process of intellectual revision is a tribute to the suppleness of the human mind and its capacity to adjust to poorly anticipated and intractable unpleasantness. People need beliefs to comfort themselves, and by the end of the 1960s deterrence had evolved into an often tangled and murky system of belief that dominated the political and psychological understanding of the nuclear age. If in some respects this was an age of science and analysis, it was also very much an age of belief, and often primitive, misguided, and illusory beliefs. An examination of the impact of these beliefs on United States policy during the late 1970s and 1980s is the principal concern of the chapter that follows.

CHAPTER THREE

Make-Believe

For some time now, the United States and Russia have been struggling not so much against each other as against phantoms ... It is not the rivalry between the United States and Russia which offers the main threat to peace. It is the irrational premises and impulses that underlie the policies of both which threaten the world with incalculable dangers.

Adam Ulam, *The Rivals*, 1971[1]

The catchy but very different titles of two books of essays on American foreign policy published only four years apart provide a political barometer of changing American sentiments on world affairs during the late 1970s and early 1980s. The first volume, published in 1979, was entitled *Eagle Entangled: United States Foreign Policy in a Complex World*. The second, which appeared in 1983 and dealt with United States foreign policy in the 1980s, was entitled *Eagle Defiant*.[2] At the end of the 1970s many Americans were frustrated, often angry, and sometimes humiliated about their nation's apparent fall from international grace; they felt "entangled" in the world in a new way – one that involved a profound sense of a loss of control. National self-esteem had been, if not battered, at least bruised – by defeat in Vietnam, by anti-American tumult in distant places (Iran in particular), by the apparent signs that the Soviet adversary was on the march and flexing its muscles, both in its military build-up and in its relations with Third World countries in Africa and southwest Asia. As the decade was ending, an academic observer, Kenneth W. Thompson, offered a summary view of American political sentiments: "The national mood is troubled, anxious, and confused. Doubt and despair are pervasive. From supreme self-confidence that for every problem a solution could be found, the national consensus on the future has fallen to a level of dread fear that national problems have outrun solutions ... As Vietnam, Watergate, and the energy problem have weakened America's image of its international role, the crisis of confidence has spread to issues of national security and the threat of a nuclear war."[3]

By contrast, during the early years of the 1980s the political mood of the United States, both in Washington and at the grass roots, was unapologetically assertive: sometimes defiant (as in dealing with the United Nations); strikingly and often stridently nationalist; resurgently anti-Soviet and sceptical of, if not hostile to, détente; and self-regarding to the point, at times, of narcissism (the 1984 Los Angeles Olympics gave full expression to these feelings). America, it was said, was back in the saddle and was again being taken seriously by the rest of the world. And in effecting this revival of the nation, nuclear weapons were allotted a role of prominence that harked back to some of the attitudes of a generation earlier.

In 1980, when Ronald Reagan was campaigning for the Republican party's presidential nomination, he had a message that growing numbers of Americans were in sympathy with. American defences, he said, had been allowed to deteriorate; Soviet military power had forged ahead; the role of the United States as a world leader had not been properly sustained; and future security would depend on rebuilding the nation's armaments and reviving its presence on the global stage. It was repeatedly asserted that the Soviet Union had achieved military, including nuclear, superiority – a superiority (in some meaningful sense) in the capacity to act destructively. As Reagan put it on one occasion: "the Soviet Union has done something that we had not counted on at all – they have surpassed us in many instances in military technology which we thought they certainly could not do in the foreseeable future."[4] Much was said concerning the prospect, perhaps even the reality, of America as Number Two. This alleged superiority of Soviet military power – a common refrain around 1980 which was sometimes represented as established fact, sometimes only as imminent – was said to be an acute present danger, and the media and political speeches were replete with gloomy forecasts and anxious warnings. The Committee on the Present Danger (established in 1976) was only one of many well-funded lobbies that helped to awaken and sustain a sense of insecurity among the general public. This was also a time when a view was taking hold that Moscow was committed, not so much to deterrence, as the United States clearly was, as to a nuclear war-fighting strategy. As Reagan remarked shortly before his election, "the Soviet Union decided some time ago that a nuclear war was possible and was winnable." To American listeners, this was obviously a dangerous not to say barbaric belief. An imposing American countervailing power was essential to dissuade the men in the Kremlin from acting on this belief: "we have to build up our deterrent capacity," thought the future president, "to the point that they never see the point at which [a nuclear war] could be won."[5] Many people shared this view.

Whether or not nuclear superiority had actually ever meant much in terms of usable political influence, the United States had certainly ceased to enjoy any significant nuclear superiority at least a decade before 1980. But during the 1970s most Americans had shown little interest in these issues. They were distracted by other pressing matters – the political morass in southeast Asia, the Watergate scandal, price inflation at home – and were for the most part content with the sort of political stability that was said to derive from nuclear deterrence. President Richard Nixon had endorsed the notion of nuclear sufficiency. Nuclear war was considered unthinkable. For a while détente seemed to be flourishing and, in many people's eyes, it offered hopeful prospects for future East-West relations. Moreover, attentive and informed citizens knew that the United States had moved ahead vigorously with MIRVing (that is, converting single-warhead missiles into multi-warhead ones, with each warhead capable of independent targeting after launch), an innovation that Moscow was not able to emulate until the mid-1970s, five years after the first American deployments. Consequently, those who needed reassurance from raw numbers could take comfort in the fact that, while Soviet nuclear delivery systems were in the same quantitative league as those of the United States (particularly long-range missiles: the American bomber force was incontestably more potent), for most of the 1970s Washington had a large numerical preponderance in strategic nuclear warheads. Indeed, it still retained that numerical superiority (for whatever it might have been worth) at the end of the decade.

The end of the 1970s was not conducive to calm assessments. The Soviet Union was deploying its own MIRVs, which meant that its warhead inventory was growing rapidly. Thus arguments that pointed to the dangerous implications and perhaps open-endedness of the Soviet arms build-up seemed especially believable. "When we build, they build; when we stop, they build": this was a snappy judgment that captured widespread American attention. In fact, neither side ever came close to stopping; and while the Americans were inclined to regard their own build-up kindly and to accept its legitimacy, they feared that the Soviet build-up might have less to do with the pursuit of parity than with the pursuit of superiority –

at least, that is what they were told again and again by many strategic analysts and defence intellectuals. The doctrinaire and heavy-handed smugness of the Brezhnev régime reinforced the plausibility of these pessimistic readings of Soviet intentions, and the Kremlin during this period certainly did little to assuage American fears. Seeing themselves as the injured party, few Americans thought a lot about the interactive nature of the nuclear rivalry, despite the strong evidence of Soviet reactiveness. As Bernard Brodie observed in 1978: "Those people who are looking so hard for the reason for the recent Soviet build-up might consider that one possibility is that their build-up was triggered by ours, and that it continues to be stimulated by [the desire] to catch up rather than clearly to surpass us."[6] Of course, no one could prove conclusively that the Soviet Union was not seeking military superiority; and as a consequence of this uncertainty, many citizens felt safer and more comfortable (and certainly more in conformity with native American traditions of anti-communism) in accepting the hardline reading of Soviet be-haviour which was loudly proclaimed during these years, a reading that denied Moscow any benefit of the doubt. Most people were not in the mood to see shades of grey.

By 1979–80 Americans were to some degree shaken – and increas-ingly disposed to fight back. Robert Kaiser, in an essay subtitled "Goodbye to Détente," published in *Foreign Affairs'* annual survey for 1980, tried to explain the deeper roots of this anxious political psychology. Americans "are uncomfortable at the thought of a world in which America is not predominant. The idea that America should naturally be by far the world's strongest military power took hold in the United States with remarkable speed and force during and after World War II. Future historians," he speculated, "will likely be stunned by the inability of contemporary American politicians to discuss frankly just how abnormal the period of great American superiority was, and how relatively easily a determined power like the u.s.s.r. could force the United States to choose between an endless, endlessly costly military competition and a world of more equally shared influence."[7]

The proposition that post-World War II American superiority might be contingent and temporary was unpalatable, perhaps even unintelligible, to many Americans. It was certainly not a view that won endorsement in Ronald Reagan's political circles. For these people, American superiority was a given, a part of the political state of nature; and to the extent that this superiority had been eroded, the erosion was a result of carelessness, lack of vigilance, and timorous liberalism (which was sometimes represented as "appeasement") and definitely not of the inescapable and impersonal pressures of history. If there was failure, it was a failure of will. Americans were still a chosen people. The Soviet Union was regarded as deeply menacing and insatiably expansionist – the invasion of Afghanistan in late 1979 was offered as fresh confirmation of the solid grounds for distrusting the Kremlin. Soviet power was believed to be fundamentally illegitimate, an evil that must be resisted, that could not be accommodated or negotiated with in any serious way. The leverage that Moscow had gained over Washington as a result of its vast military power was a deeply painful reality – a reality that was thought to have come about not so much because the Soviet Union had earned this influence by its own persistent efforts, but because previous United States policy-makers had allowed their country's military superiority to slip away and the nation's vital global interests to come under attack. The present danger was serious; the pressing problems were real; but these problems could be corrected if America would regroup, rearm, and return to its true self.

Ronald Reagan, arriving in power in 1981 on a tide of nationalist discontent, had great expectations for the nation's future. His promises were expansive, his optimism apparently unlimited. The eight years in American history over which he presided turned out to be full of surprises and interesting twists and turns, not least for the notion of security. Even more surprising, though, was what unfolded in Moscow from the mid-1980s, as the Soviet Union embarked on a journey that almost everyone at the beginning of the decade had considered unthinkable. Some of the basic premises of postwar international politics began to fray, and by 1987 many observers were coming to believe that these Cold War premises were due for a major intellectual overhaul if not actual burial. Commentators on world politics in the East or the West who spoke of the changing "correlation of forces" in the late 1980s (Soviet commentators generally found it best to avoid such language) had quite a different meaning in mind from what those words had meant only a dozen years before. One of the best-selling books in the United States in 1988 was entitled *The Rise and Fall of the Great Powers*, and from the perspective of the world's two superpowers the metaphor of "the fall" was disturbingly relevant, at least in certain respects, and more obviously so in Moscow than in Washington. If by the later 1980s Reaganite celebratory exuberance was looking excessive if not illusory, the complacency of official Soviet dogma was so transparently at odds with the country's evident malaise that it was publicly jettisoned and roundly denounced by the Soviet leadership that emerged after 1985. The greatness of the world's two greatest powers was no longer so easy to specify. And these uncertainties affected people's understanding of what was still thought of as the great deterrent: these two vast arsenals of nuclear weapons.

FOR NUCLEAR WEAPONS

The Reagan administration was deeply committed to nuclear weapons and zealously promoted their development. Much political capital was invested in marketing the MX missile (repackaged from the Carter years as the Peacekeeper) to Congress and the public, even though no plausible basing mode for it was ever devised (the 50 very expensive MX missiles eventually deployed sit immobile in former Minuteman silos). The B-1 bomber programme, which President Jimmy Carter had apparently killed, was revived and (again expensively) brought to fruition, though with rather mixed results, for several crashed and major questions were raised about the aircraft's reliability and capacity to perform as advertised. (Even after all 100 B-1s had been produced in 1988, very few were thought to be fully operational because of technical deficencies.) And in late 1988 the ultra-expensive (at least half a billion dollars a piece) successor to the B-1, the B-2 Stealth bomber, was unveiled to the public. While proclaiming his determination to reduce the size of the world's nuclear arsenals, President Reagan authorized a net average increase of several hundred strategic nuclear warheads per year. And when the need for economies started to intrude into the arms build-up during the second Reagan administration, the budgetary knife was applied disproportionately to non-nuclear military procurements and general maintenance, leaving the budgets for nuclear weapons systems comparatively protected.

These were undoubtedly prosperous years for the designers, producers, and custodians of America's nuclear deterrent. The Reagan administration was consistently hostile to any comprehensive nuclear test ban treaty, for such a treaty would have constrained future American developments in nuclear weaponry. The Arms Control and Disarmament Agency (ACDA), which had been established in the 1960s to promote restraint on weapons development and offer a counterweight to the Pentagon, was put in the hands of the champions of more weapons and the critics of arms control. And at the United Nations, virtually all significant efforts to foster disarmament were vigorously resisted by the American delegation.[8]

In the eyes of its promoters and supporters, the nuclear arms build-up of the early 1980s was necessary, entirely warranted, and long overdue. In thinking about "the threat" to American security, these people usually highlighted the size of the recent and current Soviet nuclear build-up, the immorality of the Soviet régime, which was sometimes likened to that of the Nazis, and the danger that such a powerful and immoral régime *might not be deterred*. Great power in American hands was one thing, for the United States was obviously a nation committed to peace and the preservation and enhancement of democratic values. Great power in Soviet hands, however, was seen as an entirely different matter, for the régime in the Kremlin was inherently aggressive and expansionist, acknowledged little if any moral restraint, and pursued power mostly for its own sake. In the past, it was felt, Moscow's predatory ambitions had been confronted by a strong United States (sometimes effectively, sometimes ineffectively: judgments varied), notably one that enjoyed nuclear superiority. This superiority was thought to have been a vital source of salutary discipline; to be losing it or to have already lost it boded ill for the future of freedom. Who knew what the Soviet Union might try if it no longer had to face superior American power? Perhaps its healthy respect for Washington would weaken. Perhaps it might be tempted to take greater political risks, to heighten its challenges to American interests, and to exploit the new opportunities for aggression that it was increasingly being offered – offered largely, it was felt, because of the negligence, woolly-headedness, and irresolution of American leaders.

Americans' views of what their nation ought to be doing with regard to nuclear weapons were always heavily informed by their opinions about the purposes and capacities of the Soviet Union. The political right held firm and uncompromising views on this subject, and during the late 1970s and early 1980s these views gained increased acceptance and eventually came to be fervently espoused by many officials in Washington. One such hardline reading of superpower relations appeared in early 1986, in a letter printed in *Physics Today* from Robert S. Flum, an official employed in the Space and Naval Warfare Systems Command of the Navy Department. Flum was reflecting on the nature of his country's relationship with the USSR: "I submit that, from our point of view, there is no such thing as a good political relationship with the Soviet Union. I maintain that the Soviet Union and its people ... have been at war either internally or externally for nearly 400 years. War is the norm, not the 'abnorm', for them. Such people do not consider war unusual. They are convinced, intellectually, politically and theologically, that the only way for 'Mother Russia' to be safe is for her to be totally in control of the world. All other peoples must be subservient to

'Mother Russia'." There was, then, no basis for political accommo-dation or coexistence. The Soviet Union was said to have a long historical perspective and an ultimate objective of world domination. "Eventually they expect the will of the United States to weaken and atrophy such that a Soviet takeover would be virtually bloodless." They might make the occasional tactical concession, but their long-term goal remained unchanged. Thus negotiations were hopeless. How, then, could the United States "hold off this juggernaut in our time and in the future?" There was, Flum believed, only one realistic answer to this question: "We must continue to be so armed and so prepared as to make it prohibitively expensive to the USSR to attempt to dominate the United States by force." This position might have been seen by some as simply a call to the United States to arm to the teeth; for Flum, however, the point was that only an America so armed could keep at bay the militant hostility of the enemy.[9]

This letter voiced sentiments that were widely held and certainly carried more political clout in the 1980s than they had in the decade before; and it also testified to the crucial importance in these strategic arguments of the views a person attributed to the Soviet Union. The ideological right in the United States had little doubt about the nature of the Soviet régime (it was a totalitarian dictatorship) or about the ruthlessness of its leaders and their determination to destroy Amer-ica and all it stood for. The notion of the "evil empire" had been circulating for years and winning widespread endorsement well be-fore Ronald Reagan gave these words a presidential seal of approval. Senator Barry Goldwater had presented this position in a robust fashion in his 1979 memoirs: "It is very difficult for a free people in a society rooted in the Judeo-Christian ethic to comprehend the nature of the enemy or truly to understand the incredible arsenal of weapons deployed against us. The Russians are determined to conquer the world. They will employ force, murder, lies, flattery, subversion, bribery, extortion, and treachery. Everything they stand for and believe in is a contradiction of our understanding of the nature of man. Their artful use of propaganda has anesthetized the free world. Our will to resist is being steadily eroded, and this is a contest of will."[10] Of course, some Americans felt that the Soviet Union had changed over the years and that, while still an adversary in many ways, it was behaving more like a normal great power and thus could be negotiated with. But the right had little if any use for this view. As Eugene Rostow, a prominent member of the foreign policy élite who was to become President Reagan's first director of ACDA, put it in 1977: "there has been no change in the nature of Soviet policy ... On the contrary, Soviet policy is more ominous than

at any earlier period; it is sustained by a far larger and more threatening armory, and by a political will more ruthless and more reckless
than that of Stalin. Soviet foreign policy is designed and carried out,
after all, by the same men who planned the Gulag Archipelago."[11]

Such worst-case thinking brought together a highly pessimistic
view of Soviet objectives and intentions and a highly optimistic
(some would have said vastly exaggerated) view of Soviet military
capabilities. The stature of the USSR was declared to be both imposing and contemptible. The Soviet Union was regarded simultaneously as ten feet tall with respect to its military might and a kind
of moral and spiritual midget. ("Godless communism" was a phrase
that still struck a chord in many Americans.) The ideological right
assumed the Kremlin's political intentions to be sinister. Soviet military capabilities were more open to debate, though whatever an
analyst's particular assessment might be, there was no doubt that
Soviet force levels had expanded greatly since the mid-1960s and
any prudent analyst wanted to err on the side of caution and take
care not to underestimate what damage the Soviet military could
inflict on the West, should it so choose. Those who would rarely
allow Moscow any political benefit of the doubt routinely gave it the
military benefit of the doubt, with the result that Soviet military
strengths were regularly accentuated (in fact, they were often grossly
inflated) and Soviet military weaknesses were regularly depreciated
and ignored (such as the fact that its navy had not a single large
aircraft carrier whereas the United States had fourteen). Some people
on the right conceded uncertainties and acknowledged that it was
not easy to assess the enemy's strengths or motives – after all, Western analysts were faced with trying to come to grips with a very
secretive state. All the same, the right argued, wise policy-makers
should assume if not quite the worst about the enemy then at least
a state of affairs approaching the worst. Who could say what the
Soviet Union *might* do *if* it became overly bold in response to United
States weaknesses? It was only sensible, surely, to take account of
such grim possibilities. As one strategist wrote in 1979, in a fashion
that was designed to appear moderate: "It is not necessary to believe
in the aggressive intentions of the Soviet leadership to recognize the
danger that can result if the Soviets achieve a first-strike capability;
the opportunity for political blackmail and coercion would be great.
Moreover, due to U.S. fears of a Soviet first-strike and Soviet fears
of an American preemptive attack, a crisis resulting from Soviet
attempts to obtain even limited political objectives could prove destabilizing and result in nuclear war."[12] It was important to prevent
conditions from arising that might prove irresistibly tempting to the

Kremlin and, perhaps, provoke panic or timorousness in Washington.

Many of those who were alarmed about what they called the present danger had no doubts as to the thrust of Soviet strategic policy, either before or during the Reagan years. Writing in the mid-1980s Eugene Rostow declared: "Soviet nuclear doctrine presents no particular philosophical difficulties. The Soviet Union is building its nuclear arsenal as the ultimate sanction behind a policy of indefinite expansion achieved both by intimidation and by the aggressive use of conventional force, terrorism, and subversion. Thus Soviet nuclear policy is an integral part of a broader program of aggression."[13] Elsewhere he made an even stronger claim: "In the Soviet drive for hegemony, the ultimate weapon is completely new: a nuclear first-strike capacity designed to intimidate and paralyze any resistance through the use either of conventional or of nuclear forces."[14] It was simply assumed in these circles that the Soviet Union was in pursuit of nuclear superiority; sometimes it was suggested that it had already attained it and thus might no longer be deterred. As Norman Podhoretz, editor of *Commentary* and a prominent voice on the right, remarked in 1980: "It may ... already be too late. The Soviets may think that the nuclear balance has now tipped in their favor. Or they may think that the parity which we have deliberately permitted them to achieve over the past fifteen years ... has deprived the American nuclear threat of credibility."[15] The danger was immediate; the United States would have to be woken up from its slumbers, for it was vulnerable to catastrophe in a way that it had never been before. (There was much talk at this time of a "window of vulnerability.") Restoring the credibility of the United States nuclear threat was clearly a critical priority.

This was the thinking that underlay the demands of the early 1980s for new nuclear weapons: more weapons, more survivable weapons, more threatening weapons. These demands had gained ground during the last two years of the Carter presidency, and with the arrival of the Reagan administration they really took hold in Washington. The new weapons (the build-up was usually described as "modernization") were designed, it was said, to strengthen deterrence. Their deployment would convince the Soviet Union of American resolve; convince it that aggression would be unprofitable; convince it that its war aims, presumed to be victory, could not be realized. As Robert McFarlane, one of President Reagan's numerous national security advisers, remarked toward the end of the Reagan years: "The goal of our nuclear strategy has been to convince the Soviet leaders that it would never make sense for them to initiate a strategic nuclear conflict, because of the survivability and retaliatory capacity of u.s. forces."[16] (In fact, there was no evidence that Soviet leaders had ever been *unconvinced* of these facts: the United States retained by any rational standards massive retaliatory power. However, by positing that Moscow *might* need further convincing, the conclusion would readily follow that even more weapons were required.) A rebuilt American strength, according to Reaganite thinking, would foster international stability (sadly lacking in the 1970s) and enhance the prospects for a peaceful future. An American build-up of nuclear weapons was entirely justified, for as the secretary of defense, Caspar Weinberger, observed in mid-1983: "while Soviet forces clearly exceed any responsible measure of what is needed for deterrence – ours do not."[17] The United States was in no way taking a leading role in the arms race; it was only acting defensively, in response to provocative Soviet actions. Or, as President Reagan put it in early 1985: "One nation, the Soviet Union, has conducted the greatest military buildup in the history of man, building arsenals of awesome offensive weapons."[18] The United States, under firm leadership, had to demonstrate to the Kremlin that this awesome arsenal would not be permitted to crush the spirit of free peoples.

Peace through strength: this was hardly a novel idea. Both superpowers had endorsed it, and each was in the habit of justifying its own new weapons by referring to the offensive conduct and weapons developments, real or alleged or at least perceived, of the other. There was, of course, an alternative opinion that the national interest would be best served by mutual or even unilateral restraints on armaments, restraints that would be embraced in the concept of arms control; but arms control was, if not anathema to many of the players in Reagan's Washington, then certainly a low priority and treated more as a matter of public relations than of political substance. What counted in dealing with Moscow were military power and will; diplomacy was not highly regarded (at least not until 1987–8), partly because of its traditional emphasis on compromise, accommodation, and the give-and-take of negotiation, all of which had fallen out of political favour. George Will, the prominent and well-connected political columnist, expressed a commonplace sentiment in a piece on "The Illusions of Arms Control," which appeared at the time of the Reykjavik meeting between Reagan and Mikhail Gorbachev in October 1986. "Arms control is antithetical to the raison d'être of the Soviet state," he asserted; "the only formula for security against totalitarians is to keep your powder dry – and have lots of powder."[19]

By the end of the Reagan presidency large claims were being made for the success of this robust policy. Nuclear weapons, it was said, had once again served to keep the peace; they had underlined the renewal of American strength; they had helped to make Moscow more reasonable and more attentive to American interests. According to the USAF chief of staff, Larry D. Welch, in September 1988: "Our progress to date in strategic forces modernization has reduced the risk of nuclear war and has also driven the Soviets to negotiate seriously at the arms control table."[20] The hawks felt vindicated: weaponry had made for peace; peace was a function of American military power. The strength of the United States had been restored, and the correlation of forces no longer favoured the adversary. In late 1986, Caspar Weinberger looked back upon six years of defence strategy and was satisfied with what had happened: "In 1980 the crucial issue was whether the United States could afford to acquiesce in the Soviet Union's attempt to achieve a position of global military superiority. The answer from the American electorate was clear. We agreed to pay the price for military strength to deter war."[21] Many Americans would not have agreed with this latter claim; however, while the disposition to raise revenue to pay for strength may have been feeble, the disposition of the administration to spend on weapons – indeed, to spend at extraordinary peacetime levels – was never in doubt.

American nuclear weapons, it was said again and again in the 1980s, were intended *to deter*. Whenever a new nuclear weapons system was being promoted, the argument almost always was that it would enhance deterrence; that it would strengthen the defensive posture of the West; that it would in some way make us more secure. Virtually all major weapons procurements during these years were justified on the grounds that they would promote deterrence and thus, of course, stability and peace. What was usually not clear were the specifics. How exactly would deterrence work in practice? What were the logical connections between the political ends (war avoidance) and the military means (weapons for war)? Was the meaning of deterrence clear or did it mean different things to different people? Some of these matters are explored in the following chapter. For the moment we can confine ourselves to two observations.

First, nuclear weapons were often treated primarily as symbols of power and as tokens of political determination. They were bearers of important messages: expressions of resolve, statements to the world that the United States would no longer allow itself to be pushed around. General Bennie L. Davis, the head of SAC, advanced

this line of argument in late 1981: "By setting in motion the production lines to develop the MX missiles and the B-1 bomber ... we
are sending a crucial message to friends and foes alike: America
stands ready to take whatever steps are necessary to protect its vital
interests at home and abroad."[22] Appearances counted; it was vital
that the world perceive that the United States was resolute and truly
deserved its reputation as a superpower; and nuclear weapons were
potent enhancers of this political credibility. A nuclear arms build-
up was said to be one important way of influencing perceptions in
a positive manner. (Nikita Khrushchev had undoubtedly had such
notions in mind when, a quarter-century before, he had staged his
various rocket-rattling theatrics.) In the second Reagan administration, when questions about the utility of this build-up and whether
the country was getting proper value for all the money being spent
became more insistent, these sceptics were likely to confront arguments from the other side that emphasized the importance of perceptions. One strategic writer in 1986 proposed that the mere fact
of building weapons had deterrent value because of how these procurements were politically perceived: "It is in influencing these perceptions that the Reagan-Weinberger buildup has had its major
impact to date. The chief U.S. foes and allies, as well as the U.S.
Congress and the American electorate, are convinced that the United
States under Reagan is determined to strengthen greatly its defense
posture ... The belief that the United States is more determined to
defend itself, and its allies, has doubtless contributed to deterrence
in the 1980s."[23] Whatever the objective reality, inducing others to
believe what you wanted them to believe (that is, that the United
States was resolute) was a critical priority and a central purpose in
deploying nuclear weapons.

Such arguments placed exceptional stress on the subjective components of deterrence, whatever the actual balance of forces, and
on the importance of being seen to be strong, whatever weaknesses
closer inspection might reveal. A reputation for strength was crucial.
And nuclear weaponry was a vital and visible currency of power.
In mid-1985, James Schlesinger, secretary of defense under Richard
Nixon and Gerald Ford, dealt with the charge that the Reagan administration "has no *specific* foreign policy monuments to its name" in
the following manner: "It does have one generic accomplishment,
a vital one: it has restored America's international prestige and the
perception of American power. In foreign policy, that is immensely
important – and can compensate for a significant number of blunders
elsewhere."[24]

My second observation presses in a different direction, for the new nuclear weapons of the 1980s were not just for show. Although it was sometimes alleged that they were not intended to be used and were only designed to intimidate (or, more politely, to deter), elaborate military plans were of course in place that called for their use in all sorts of contingencies. Nuclear weapons were produced and deployed, not exactly with the intention and certainly not with the hope of using them, but definitely with use in mind: use on the battlefield, use to achieve military objectives, use in fighting a war and perhaps prevailing in war. War plans existed; these war plans called for the destruction of thousands of enemy targets; and the best way to destroy these targets was with nuclear warheads. These war plans, in short, generated a huge demand for new nuclear weapons. Richard Halloran, a writer on national security affairs for the *New York Times*, pointed to these realities in a report of December 1986. He noted: "The Reagan Administration's policy of being prepared for protracted nuclear warfare demands forces far larger than those needed for one retaliatory strike. The forces must be able to survive sustained attacks with enough warheads to fire back repeatedly. The Administration wants to be able to destroy Soviet leaders in their sanctuaries and Soviet nuclear forces, conventional forces and war industry, more targets than previous Administrations envisioned."[25] More targets implied more nuclear weapons, the most effective destroyers of targets. Here, then, was another justification for the priority that Washington placed on the nuclear arms build-up.

This was a quite different goal from massive retaliation, a capability which is in fact rather easy to achieve and which can be achieved with relatively few weapons and was therefore not particularly interesting from a military point of view. Over the years, and well before the 1980s, the Pentagon had become more and more attached to counterforce strategies – that is, strategies that emphasized the destruction of military targets – and as new technologies made weapons much more accurate and therefore supposedly more discriminating, military planning came to centre on "flexible" nuclear use (sometimes referred to as "graduated deterrence" or "escalation dominance") and on eliminating Soviet military assets *before* they could be used. These assets encompassed a wide range of targets, including missile silos, air bases, troop concentrations, naval forces, defence industries, communication and transportation links, and command and control centres. Because the number of targets was substantial, only a large and up-to-date arsenal could properly cover them. Every new nuclear weapons system would have its role to play in the overall scheme of things. Thus when the B-2 Stealth

bomber was given its public unveiling in November 1988, the secretary of the air force, Edward C. Aldridge, Jr, reportedly said that
"the B-2 would be especially effective in pin-pointing high value
targets. He did not specify which targets these are, but the Air Force
Chief of Staff, Gen. Larry D. Welch, disclosed last week that targets
could include senior Soviet leaders in underground bunkers." Bombers were thought to be especially well-suited for this search-and-
destroy mission. Mr Aldridge added "that 'the capability of holding
those things at risk that the Soviets value' is at the heart of deterrent
strategy, and that the B-2 was 'essential' for this role."[26]

Because the Soviet Union valued many things, a lot had to be
targeted if these things were to be truly at risk. And because the
Soviet Union was continually striving to make some of these targets
less vulnerable by hardening them or concealing them or making
them mobile, the United States was said by nuclear theorists and
military planners to need smarter and more sophisticated weapons
to counteract these developments. Of course, these weapons would
only be used and the war plans would only be implemented "if
deterrence failed" – and the stated purpose of all this weaponry was
to ensure that deterrence did not fail. But if it did fail and if nuclear
war did break out, then the quality and quantity of forces in being
were considered by the military to be of the first importance. If
"ultimate degrees of nuclear weaponry are employed" in the event
of major war, General Davis asserted in 1982, "the size and strength
of our weapons and the comprehensive planning of target selection
and weapon lay-down will determine the extent to which it is possible for our society to emerge from such conflict with advantage
and [be] able to control its destiny."[27] The air force's objective, in
short, would be for the United States to survive and in some meaningful sense not to lose the third world war.

AGAINST NUCLEAR
WEAPONS

"We seek the total elimination, one day, of nuclear weapons from
the face of the earth": these words were spoken by President Reagan
in his second inaugural address, in January 1985.[28] This ambitious
objective received presidential endorsement on numerous other oc-
casions. Despite presiding over a determined build-up of nuclear
weapons and surrounding himself with assiduously pro-nuclear advisers, Reagan frequently presented himself as a radical disarmer,
a foe of weapons of mass destruction, an actual abolitionist. One
well-informed scholar, reviewing Reagan's foreign policy in early
1989, spoke of the retiring president's "deep animus toward nuclear

weapons and the deterrent arrangements to which these weapons have given rise."[29] Reagan had been loath to accept such notions as the balance of terror and the mutuality of assured destruction (usually known more benignly as mutual deterrence), and he doubted that this state of political existence was the route to peace and stability. He thought that there must be a better way. He was concerned to find a way out of the perilous condition of nuclear vulnerability. His chosen path to a better future was, of course, the Strategic Defense Initiative (SDI) (popularly known as Star Wars). In his celebrated speech of 23 March 1983, he proposed that the United States seek to "intercept and destroy [Soviet] strategic ballistic missiles before they reached our own soil or that of our allies." He called for a vigorous commitment of scientific enterprise in order, as he put it, to discover "the means of rendering these nuclear weapons impotent and obsolete."[30]

Reagan's enthusiasm for SDI seems to have been rooted in two fundamental beliefs. The first was his sense of revulsion in the face of the *defencelessness* of the United States. He believed his country was, in a fundamental way, at the mercy of the enemy, and he found this condition unnatural and intolerable – and probably unnecessary. The United States had a right to be secure. And that security should rest not on the insecurity of mutual deterrence but on a genuine capacity for self-defence. Secondly, Reagan had a deep faith in the ability of American science and technology to produce the means to achieve this self-defence. Just as he was buoyant about the future of the United States, so too he was buoyant about the prospect of tapping the genius of American enterprise and science to overcome the nuclear peril. These were the two dominant premises that informed his public statements on strategic defence. Even before he became president he was wrestling with these issues. In an interview during his party's primary campaigns in 1980, he remarked on how he had learned during a visit to the headquarters of the North American Aerospace Defence Command in Colorado that "we couldn't do anything to stop the missiles" that the Soviet Union could fire at his country. "I think the thing that struck me was the irony that here, with this great technology of ours ... we cannot stop any of the weapons that are coming at us. I don't think there's been a time in history when there wasn't a defense against some kind of thrust, even back in the old-fashioned days when we had coast artillery that would stop invading ships if they came."[31]

During the first two years of his presidency, Reagan received counsel on these matters from only a handful of advisers who were fervently devoted to the cause of defending against Soviet nuclear attack and they persuaded him that such defences were feasible, likely to succeed, and very much worth pursuing.[32] These men were all technological optimists; they were remarkably confident in themselves and in what science could achieve when creative people who enjoyed solid public support set their minds to the task at hand. President Reagan was readily disposed to share this enthusiasm and hold out to his nation a vision of a better future. Let us "embark," he said in his speech of March 1983, "on a program to counter the awesome Soviet missile threat with measures that are defensive. Let us turn to the very strengths in technology that spawned our great industrial base and that have given us the quality of life we enjoy today."[33] Three years later this confidence remained undiminished. In his State of the Union message of February 1986, he actually raised the rhetorical ante. Reagan assured his people that "the same technology transforming our lives can solve the greatest problem of the 20th Century. A security shield can one day render nuclear weapons obsolete and free mankind from the prison of nuclear terror. America met one historic challenge and went to the moon. Now, America must meet another – to make our strategic defense real for all the citizens of Planet Earth."[34]

Such technological exuberance had deep roots in American culture and, in fact, was a major contributor to the continuing arms race with the Soviet Union. One of the first books ever written about the military implications of atomic weapons, William Borden's *There Will Be No Time: The Revolution in Strategy* (1946), had embraced this optimistic view of technology. Borden, a young man recently back from the war, felt that "the atomic-bomb project leaves a strong inference that science, if fertilized with enthusiasm and unlimited funds, can almost produce on demand." Science was suddenly at the very centre of world politics. "The struggle for power will go on as before," Borden predicted, "but, instead of focusing on chunks of territory vital to yesterday's strategy, the important competition will take place between laboratories."[35] Forty years later the Strategic Defense Initiative was being driven by similar assumptions and a similar faith in technical solutions to political problems. In a 1987 article that pleaded for SDI, Caspar Weinberger asserted that "today, more than ever, the Western democracies must join together and take advantage of the creativity and innovation that freedom spawns." SDI would allow the West to play from strength in its rivalry with the Soviet Union. It was the "technological prowess of the West, combined with the innovative application of resources that is possible in free societies, [that] will ensure its survival."[36] Earlier, in October 1986, the editor of *U.S. News & World Report* had expressed his confidence that SDI held out the hope of "insured survivability" and recorded his opinion that it clearly deserved congressional support. "We must recognize," he concluded, "that it may be only the gleaming wings of science, coupled with reason, that can beat away the return of the Stone Age."[37]

The Strategic Defense Initiative, as conceived and communicated by the president and some of those close to him, was a visionary proposal. This vision had been shaped with little regard for informed opinion or relevant past experience;[38] and it bore virtually no relation to those realities – physical, technological, political, financial – that were known to stand in the way of such a vision being realized. Most of the analyses and feasibility studies that were conducted after March 1983 left the president's vision in shreds. But this (mostly devastating) criticism had no discernible effect on Reagan, who continued to be deeply attached to his vision; and the critics of SDI had only a modest impact on the thinking of most ordinary Americans, who tended to sympathize with their president's call for an effective security shield (some Americans were surprised to be told that no defences in fact existed) and to feel that no harm could come from striving to protect their country against nuclear attack. For the most part SDI played well on main street: it had a hopeful, positive resonance; and it was compatible with common-sense notions about how the world ought to be ordered. As was so often the case, President Reagan was closely in touch with the dreams and yearnings of his compatriots.

Whatever the critics of SDI might say, then, and however sound their arguments might be on grounds of science, logic, and evidence, the presidential vision enjoyed considerable political success. Elizabeth Drew, the Washington correspondent for the *New Yorker*, remarked on one of the reasons for this success. "The fundamental question that Reagan posed – Wouldn't it be better to have a world in which the great powers could rely on defenses, and not point offensive weapons at each other? – has a simple appeal. It is the sort of question that makes those who raise doubts risk being labelled tired and negative thinkers."[39] To many citizens SDI was a source of encouragement; it was a pre-eminently American vision (ambitious, humane, generously conceived), endorsed by a popular president, and hence worthy of support. One former high-level Pentagon official reflected on the appeal of Reagan's "pure vision" (as he called it): "This is a president who is well attuned to the American viscera. Somewhere in the American viscera we don't want to believe that some son-of-a-bitch on the other side can destroy us, and he's offering us that wonderful defense-in-the-sky. It has nothing to do with military planning; anybody who takes a serious look at this knows that the Reagan vision is unattainable ... I think you have to treat SDI not in terms of rational military planning; it's just this gut reaction that comes from the deepest, deepest recesses of the American viscera that Reagan is attuned with."[40]

The Strategic Defense Initiative certainly drew some of its sustenance from the messianic strands in American culture, the sense of a unique national mission. It was also sustained by the tradition of American exceptionalism and the belief that the unusual degree of freedom in the United States led to a special capacity for a kind of transcendence – a liberation from the constraints that bind lesser nations. SDI held out the prospect that the world could be remade; it proposed that the mutuality of vulnerability could be overcome; it hinted at a new scientific revolution that could undo that of nuclear physics; and it promised that the United States could, in a sense, turn the clock back and regain the ability to defend itself and that it could do this by itself, regardless of what others thought or did. SDI was a way for the United States to regain control of its destiny, to breathe new life into the idea of freedom (after years during which freedom had been under attack), and to repeal the cruel dilemmas and vulnerability embedded in nuclear deterrence. The United States, according to this line of thinking, should not have to come to terms with the perils of the nuclear age; rather, it should strive to escape from them and to find a (perhaps permanent) solution to the nuclear threat.

SDI advocates commonly looked at the world in this evangelical manner. According to Daniel O. Graham, a retired army general and one of the leading enthusiasts for active defences: "We can *escape* the brooding menace of 'balance of terror' doctrines by deploying defensive systems in space."[41] Norman Podhoretz thought that SDI "really does hold out the rational hope of an eventual *escape* from the threat of nuclear war."[42] Even Zbigniew Brzezinski, who had been national security adviser to President Carter, spoke (though not specifically with reference to SDI) of the United States potentially enjoying "the *immunity* that accrues to the status of a great power."[43] Such language was symptomatic of the extraordinary standards of security that some prominent Americans still assumed to be appropriate for their country. In 1985 James Schlesinger offered an unsentimental judgment of his nation's expectations: "We in the United States have been even more inclined than the Soviets to believe in the unilateral capacity to achieve *perfect* defense ... The American psyche believes that perfect defense *should* be attainable. In that we differ from all other nations. It is this unique belief that underlies the current hope for SDI."[44]

The fact of nuclear stalemate, which was the consequence of some four decades of arms racing, was a deeply frustrating condition of political existence for the American right, and part of the appeal of SDI was that it promised a way out of this military straitjacket. A properly defended America would be one with more room for manoeuvre, with more freedom of action. It would be able to pursue its purposes to better effect. Moreover, to defend oneself was a moral act, much more so, it was argued, than the act of massive retaliation. The United States, as an inherently peaceful nation – "While we need to have the power to deter the Soviets from attacking or intimidating the West," wrote Richard Nixon in 1988, "Moscow knows very well that it has no need to deter us"[45] – was fully justified in seeking ways to protect itself against aggression, and aggression was seen as an all-too-likely possibility in a world that included the Soviet Union. This was a common view among SDI's supporters, one of the most influential and zealous of whom was the military scientist and staunch anti-communist, Edward Teller. In his 1987 book, *Better a Shield Than a Sword*, Teller represented defence as a moral imperative. "Every helpful means is needed for the attempt to destroy weapons attacking the innocent – lasers, rockets, small nuclear weapons, or any other effective device. And every moral nation should be cooperatively engaged in making that attempt. Aggression is wrong, whether carried out by bow and arrow or by the hydrogen bomb. Defense is right, whether it uses a stream of particles or the concentrated energy locked in the atomic nucleus." He called for an "agreement on the morality of self-defense." "Without such an agreement," he feared, "we cannot count on the survival of the society that holds moral values so strongly that it calls them human rights."[46] Moral fervour of this sort, which was sometimes tied to fundamentalist beliefs, was occasionally evident as well in the works of nuclear planners and serving military officers.[47]

At the end of the 1980s SDI was still partly alive, though what it might actually involve (lasers and other directed-energy weapons were being superseded, it seemed, by "smart rocks" and "brilliant pebbles") and what it might be able to do in practice (assuming that it would ever be able to do much at all) were by no means clear to the attentive observer. Perhaps SDI will be seen, in retrospect, as an insignificant blip on the historical screen. Perhaps future observers will look back on it as a bizarre sideshow in the international politics of the late twentieth century. No completely firm judgments were possible at the time of writing. However, one could discern four fairly clear features of both the Strategic Defense Initiative and the arguments surrounding it.

First of all, much of the debate over SDI during the 1980s was a replay of the anti-ballistic missile debates of the late 1960s. Many of the same issues were at stake; many of the same arguments were thought to be relevant; much of the strategic logic regarding offence versus defence remained unchanged. Some of the leading roles were played by the same actors: Edward Teller, for example, energetically promoted both ABM and SDI. In the 1980s strenuous efforts were made by SDI's supporters to highlight the defensive possibilities of various new technologies: scientific advances and technical breakthroughs, they argued, offered opportunities unavailable fifteen or twenty years before. The dynamic of technology, they declared, held out the prospect of a more hopeful, securely defended future. Such technological optimism, which was an article of faith among many military strategists in the 1980s, had been characteristic of ABM supporters in the 1960s.

The criticisms of SDI drew upon much of the same logic as the criticisms of ABM. First, there were doubts about the viability of defence in the nuclear age. In the past defence had always involved attrition; but in the nuclear age attrition was meaningless, for any leakage in the event of a nuclear attack would almost certainly be catastrophic. Meaningful defence against a nuclear offence meant a virtually perfect defence, and this hardly seemed realistic in a world of Murphy's Law and other inconveniences, such as computers that were bound to err. Second, there was the virtual certainty that any defences would be vulnerable to offensive saturation. Defensive systems could simply be overwhelmed by an offensive build-up. (In the late 1960s the United States had contingency plans for just such a massive build-up in the event that the Soviet Union deployed an ABM system.)[48] Moreover, adding to the destructiveness of the offence was almost sure to be cheaper and technically easier than designing, producing, and deploying an exceptionally elaborate and super-complicated system of defence (causing something complicated to function properly was inherently more difficult than causing it to malfunction). Third, and following from these circumstances, new defensive systems were bound to elicit new offensive systems, and thus any attempts to achieve arms control were bound to be seriously impeded and possibly blocked altogether. The consequence, it was predicted, would be an intensified arms race, with defence systems provoking yet other offensive systems. Fourth, any unilateral defensive system would be vulnerable to countermeasures: to efforts by the other side to outwit or circumvent or destroy pre-emptively whatever defences were put up. Defending against a potent enemy was not analogous to getting to the moon: the moon could neither shoot back nor conceal itself nor jump out of the way. Whereas inanimate nature could not *feel* threatened, a political rival could; and in such a state of mind this rival was likely to react unco-operatively, perhaps, if the past was any guide, even defiantly. And such defiance could be readily manifested politically in all sorts of unwelcome ways.

These fundamental issues were of much more importance than all the arcane technical details that sometimes flooded and obscured the public debate on SDI. They had been discussed rather fully in the 1960s but were aired once again in the 1980s, with the addition of very few new ideas. Old arguments were repeated. Propositions exposed as fallacies in an earlier generation and dismissed from consideration were resurrected in the 1980s and had to be fought over and defeated a second time. Claims that had already been discredited had to be scrutinized and discredited again.[49] Perhaps the only major new factor in the 1980s was presidential will. For whatever science and informed analysis might conclude, the world had little choice but to heed the desires of an American head of state. And this particular president had put his formidable political weight behind SDI; he consistently treated it with special favour; and he never showed any doubts about the merits of his vision.[50] As a presidential priority, SDI was bound to command political centre stage, regardless of its intrinsic merits or plausibility.

Secondly, it was soon clear that the SDI proposal had major implications for the offence, not just for the supposed defence. Whatever its promoters might say in public about America's benign intentions and the strictly defensive purposes of the project, the fact was that many of the technologies of SDI, if actually developed, *could* be used for first strikes and pre-emptive attacks. This was hardly surprising. Anything that produces large amounts of energy can be used for various tasks, one of which is attack: whether such attack would be deemed aggressive or defensive was likely to lie largely if not entirely in the eyes of the beholder. SDI technologies with offensive possibilities included anti-satellite weaponry (which was widely regarded as highly destabilizing), numerous spin-offs that would improve the efficiency of existing nuclear and non-nuclear forces, and means for striking from space against targets on earth.[51] Moreover, any supposed defence that "worked" – that is, a defence that might rebuff some of an enemy's attack – would work best if paired with a strong offensive capability that could be used pre-emptively. Insiders were well aware of this strategic logic. As William Broad, a writer on space technology for the *New York Times*, reported in December 1987: "In private, some Star Wars advocates say space-based antimissile systems can be viewed as exclusively offensive, given that a leaky shield would work best for fending off a foe's ragged retaliation after a first strike destroyed as many enemy nuclear weapons as possible. But they argue that the West – which is fundamentally pacific, is tired of building nuclear missiles, and is interested mainly in making money and satisfying creature comforts – needs to hold this offensive threat over the Soviet Union, which is backward, paranoid and expansionist."[52]

For some military planners, then, SDI was first and foremost a venture, not to render nuclear weapons impotent and obsolete, but to pursue superiority in the new frontier of space. Soviet-American military rivalry had reached a stalemate on earth, and the best terrain for restoring American superiority was beyond the earth's atmosphere. It was "out there" that the Soviet menace could be countered advantageously. Two air force officers, writing in 1981 in the *Naval War College Review*, put this priority clearly. It was essential, they said, "to engage the Soviets aggressively in a race for the high ground of space in order to secure for ourselves a position of space superiority that can provide the bedrock for our future security doctrine."[53] According to two other USAF officers, who also presented their views in the early 1980s, "Space constitutes America's best opportunity ... to get out in front of and shape what will eventually become *the decisive arena of military competition*."[54] These goals were quite different from those that President Reagan espoused. However, they were entirely consistent with the strong American tradition of technological exuberance with regard to national security. Space systems, declared the secretary of the air force in 1987, "contribute so significantly to U.S. security and defense precisely because of the U.S. technological edge, which must be aggressively preserved. That technological lead is the key to success, and the reason why the United States is second to no one in space."[55] Assertions that the Soviet Union was ahead in space weaponry, assertions designed for consumption by the general public, were almost entirely without foundation. As William Broad observed in early 1988: "at times, despite a tendency to point to the Russians, American military officials concede that the West has the edge and argue that it should be pushed to the limit. As ... Weinberger put it in a speech last year calling for rapid 'Star Wars' deployment: 'We must seize this opportunity.'"[56]

The question of how the Soviet Union could respond or would respond to United States anti-missile technologies provides a third feature of the SDI debate. In fact, SDI's supporters handled it in different ways, depending in part on the political circumstances of the moment and the audiences they were addressing. One common approach was to ignore the issue, to give it no serious consideration. Indeed, there was a remarkable degree of apparent indifference to possible hostile Soviet reactions – active countermeasures or an accelerated offensive build-up, for example. Some SDI proponents seemed almost not to care much how Moscow might react, so confident were they of the rightness of their cause and the potential efficacy of their weapons. Edward Teller, for example, simply declined to address the issue, apparently preferring to confine himself to other, more appealing matters. Caspar Weinberger at least acknowledged, as he put it, that there were arguments circulating that "efforts by one side or the other to expand and improve defenses will be accompanied by the development of more offensive weapons designed to defeat the new defenses," but he then flatly declared that "an effective defense, such as the one envisioned by the president, could not be countered in this way."[57] Whatever SDI would eventually generate, it certainly fostered in the 1980s some remarkably dogmatic thinking.

Other SDI supporters argued that, even if SDI heightened the superpower military rivalry (at least for a while), the United States could only benefit from this competition for dominance in space. The fragile Soviet economy would be placed under even more severe pressure. The Kremlin would be forced to spend huge sums in an effort to cope with SDI and consequently would have to forgo other projects. And the much more innovative and productive American economy would generate superior space-based weapons, with the result that Washington would regain some of the political-strategic advantage that it had lost during the 1960s and 1970s. This was a common hardline perspective. To confront the Soviet Union on the playing field of advanced technology was to force it on the defensive, to compel it to contend with a strengthened United States, and thus to thwart whatever aggressions it might have in mind.[58] Here was yet another expression of the assumption that the United States could, if it really wanted to, stay ahead in the arms race and derive political advantage from new military technologies. Of course, not everyone was prepared to accept this assumption. As Robert Tucker observed in 1984: "our superiority has not prevented the inferior party from duplicating our technological achievements in weapons, often within a very brief period. On more than one occasion, this duplication has also been carried out with a vengeance. There is no apparent reason to conclude that on this occasion the Soviet Union would prove unable to do what it has done with regularity in the past. Having sacrificed so much to reach its present position of strategic eminence, it may be expected to remain willing to make the necessary effort and sacrifice to keep this position."[59]

Yet another group of SDI proponents accepted the possibility of a hostile Soviet response, but held that Moscow would thereby be encouraged (or perhaps compelled) to collaborate with Washington in making a mutual transition to a defence-dominated world. Perhaps, this argument ran, SDI was indeed a sort of throwing down of the gauntlet; but there was reason to hope that the Kremlin would respond by agreeing to a "co-operative defensive transition." SDI would be a stimulus to arms control and Soviet restraint, not to further arms racing. One prominent strategist and military adviser, Colin Gray, put the case as follows: "The Soviet Union will agree to reduce its offensive threat if it calculates that in the absence of legal constraints the United States will proceed to deploy a strategic force posture – offense and defense – that will diminish Soviet security nonmarginally. What this means is that Soviet leaders will need to believe that their offense will not fare very well against a maturing U.S. SDI and that their defense will not cope very well with modernized U.S. offensive forces. Even if Soviet leaders should anticipate being able to sustain a rough equality in the strategic arms competition, still they could well decide that negotiated arms control ... would be in their best interest."[60] (No reason was proposed for thinking that Soviet leaders might define their nation's interest in this way.) A similar argument was advanced by Fred C. Iklé, a senior official in the Pentagon during the Reagan presidency. He suggested two complementary approaches to strategic defences: "We should energetically seek Soviet cooperation, since it would greatly ease and speed the transformation [to a reliance on defensive systems]. But we must also be prepared to persist on the harder road, where the Soviet Union would try as long as possible to overcome our defenses, and would resist meaningful reductions in offensive forces. The better prepared we are and the more capable of prevailing on the hard road, the more likely it is that the Soviet Union will join us on the easy road [of co-operation]."[61]

The kernel of sense in this position was the acknowledgment of the importance of Soviet co-operation. Indeed, as many critics of SDI had already pointed out, without such superpower co-operation, that is, without some kind of mutual rearrangement of the underpinnings of each nation's security, it was virtually inconceivable that unilateral American defences, deployed in the face of Soviet hostility and resistance, could be in any sense effective in enhancing the security of the American people. Only true dreamers could believe in the pure vision of SDI, as enunciated by Ronald Reagan: and while Gray and Iklé diligently promoted most of the president's military causes, they and others of like ideological mind (who, it should be recalled, were at or near the centres of power in Reagan's Washington) were perhaps a little more attuned than he was to some of the awkward facts of the real world. All the same, their views were hard to take seriously, for several reasons.

First, while seemingly hoping for or even anticipating Soviet co-operation, these strategists actually held to an exceptionally grim view of all things Soviet, a view that embraced a virtually demonic image of their adversary. And yet, when promoting SDI, they posited a remarkable transformation of Soviet conduct, from one extreme (intense hostility and brutality) to the other (co-operation on American terms). In other words, their scenario for future superpower relations, when sketched in these co-operative terms, was premised on an almost miraculous alteration in the character of the Soviet régime, brought about by pressure from Washington. Deeply pessimistic about the Soviet present and past, they offered an optimistic vision of the Soviet régime's conduct in the future and of its amenability to such challenging and well-considered American initiatives. It is hard to avoid the thought that there must be something amiss somewhere in such an implausible analysis.

Second, while gesturing towards the virtue of co-operation, these strategists were primarily interested in preserving the superpower competition: that is, in using advanced technology to continue the geopolitical struggle with the USSR and to further the global interests of the United States, which were assumed to be largely different from and opposed to those of the Soviet Union. If some new weapons were "destabilizing" (as arms controllers said of SDI), so be it. As Fred Iklé wrote in 1986: "the nature of modern Leninism forces upon us a continuing competition – a demanding, dangerous, fierce competition. And we cannot compete effectively if we exclusively pursue the ideal of stability."[62]

Third, in these strategists' minds, the co-operation of the Soviet Union was to be achieved, essentially, by compelling its acquiescence by means of vigorous competition. Moscow would thereby discover that its interests lay in accepting the new American agenda. Little or no allowance was made for other, more probable, Soviet reactions to such a challenge: perhaps defiance, possibly an accelerated Soviet nuclear arms build-up (to overwhelm any United States defences), probably countermeasures to undermine any unilateral defence (such as more sea-based cruise missiles, orbiting space mines, and anti-satellite weapons). The notion that the Kremlin would become more amenable to reason as a result of American displays of force and resolve was a revival of the ideas current in the early days of the Cold War: for some strategists of the 1980s, SDI was a welcome way to revitalize this competitive imperative. In their minds, superpower co-operation was not all that different from American pre-eminence.

Finally, it is clear that SDI could be all things to all people and that this was a major reason for its political success. The proposal took a lot of steam out of the peace movement which had burgeoned in 1982, for conceptually it seemed to accept the protesters' doubts about nuclear deterrence and endorse a more moral and less threatening strategy for ensuring security in the future. For many citizens, SDI was intelligible, appealing (who could argue against the wisdom of self-defence?), humane, and sensible; and if their well-liked president was confident of its feasibility, perhaps it deserved public support. Maybe SDI really was a way out of the dilemmas of the nuclear age. As for the experts and insiders, few of them believed in Reagan's vision; indeed, most probably thought it preposterous. However, many of them signed on as supporters of SDI, though not necessarily with the same objectives in mind as those of their president. As the former senior Pentagon official who spoke of Reagan's "pure vision" (pp 69–70) had also observed, in actual fact "the Department of Defense, which falls in line behind its commander-in-chief, has resurrected an advanced form of the Safeguard [the proposed ABM system of the late 1960s], which is to say we protect our missile fields. And that's a little different from protecting our people and population."[63] Official communications about SDI came to speak more and more about enhancing deterrence, not about protecting people. For these officials and military consultants, SDI did not imply any serious search for an escape from nuclear deterrence, which they did not believe possible. Rather, it implied business as usual: a continuing "modernization" of nuclear weapons systems; renewed efforts to protect some of these systems (especially immobile ones on land); healthy military budgets; and, for the major aerospace corporations, attractive opportunities for lucrative and long-term contracts. Many established interests stood to benefit from SDI, and given its extraordinary open-endedness and indefiniteness, they might reasonably expect (they hoped) to get these benefits for decades to come.

To the foes and detractors of arms control, who were well placed in Reagan's Washington to work their wills, especially the civilians in the Pentagon, the pursuit of SDI came to be valued as an effective impediment to diplomatic negotiations. The Soviet authorities were bound to reject any strategic arms control proposals that insisted that SDI be permitted to forge freely ahead in violation of the 1972 ABM Treaty, which was what the president appeared determined should occur. Thus SDI became a convenient monkey wrench to throw into the process of seeking agreements with the other side (though Reagan himself may not have thought this way). Once such incompatible negotiating positions were permitted to materialize, one of the prime objectives of the hardliners – to hold back or even sabotage arms control – could be more readily accomplished. And as an added attraction, from their point of view, the unwelcome constraints of the ABM Treaty would be undermined and perhaps eventually rendered obsolete.

Some people saw SDI as a many-faceted and promising venture. For others the proposal was alive with contradictions and untested technological theories. Certainly SDI did foster numerous new technological visions and work on new technologies, whose consequences or utility could not, of course, be clearly foreseen. No doubt some of these technologies would turn out to have some sort of application for something some day. Whether any of them would serve to deliver the country from the perils of the nuclear age was a different matter.[64]

SMOKE AND MIRRORS

The two volumes of essays mentioned at the beginning of this chapter were followed by a third collection in 1987 entitled *Eagle Resurgent? The Reagan Era in American Foreign Policy.* "Resurgent" was certainly an apt designation and in tune with the Reagan White House's representation of the flow of history. The United States, according to this view, was making a comeback; it was once again strong and determined and respected; and it was pressing resolutely against the expansive drive of communism and forcing it to retreat. The American public, it was widely agreed, was enjoying a renewed self-confidence and faith in the nation's future. Anxieties about their nation's place as Number One had been largely laid to rest – at least in the eyes of the media and most electors. In the mid-1980s national self-celebration (as expressed, for example, in the 1986 Statue of Liberty commemoration) was regularly on display. But doubts persisted, and it was significant that this book of essays had a question mark after "resurgent" in its title. Was the country actually revitalized? Was it really regaining its grip on the course of history? Were there solid and lasting achievements that could be pointed to? These were questions that would not go away and in fact were being raised even more insistently during the later Reagan years, especially, perhaps, with regard to the issue of national security.

The promoters and publicists of the Reagan "revolution" usually put special stress on matters of social psychology: that is, on public morale and confidence, on positive feelings and strength of will. This concern for subjectivity as against objective realities was a common refrain in the ascendant ideology that President Reagan both espoused and symbolized. George Shultz, the secretary of state, firmly endorsed this outlook in 1985: "the most important new way of thinking that is called for in this decade is our way of thinking about ourselves. Civilizations thrive when they believe in themselves; they decline when they lose this faith. All civilizations confront massive problems, but a society is more likely to master its challenges, rather than be overwhelmed by them, if it retains this bedrock self-confidence that its values are worth defending. This is the essence of the Reagan revolution and of the leadership the President has sought to provide in America."[65] Believing in America: this was at the heart of the president's appeal. Belief fostered strength, and strength made for the national resurgence that was said to be under way. Claims that all was well – or at least becoming well – were commonplace. In early 1987, Kenneth Adelman, the director of ACDA, was commenting on the state of Soviet-American relations and concluded that "the broad trend since 1981 has been toward more stable relations because of *renewed American strength and self-confidence*; our central task is to preserve this trend, with or without new [arms control] agreements."[66] Diplomatic accords such as arms control were (at best) of secondary importance; what really counted for a peaceful future was the preservation of a strong and vibrant United States.

A strong nation meant a determined and assertive America, one that had regained its competitive edge in the world of power politics. From this angle of vision, the pursuit of accommodation and conciliation was decidedly less important than the pursuit of advantage at the expense of one's adversary. The rivalry with Moscow should be pursued with vigour; restraints ought not to be welcomed; and given the fundamental values and geopolitical interests at stake, priority should be given to ensuring the success of the United States in this struggle. Such sentiments were hardly conducive to arms control or any sort of superpower détente. Late in 1986, Fred Iklé published an article entitled "The Idol of Stability," which called into question the feasibility – even the desirability – of stability in the relationship between his government and that of the Soviet Union, especially in arms control. "Perhaps," he thought, "the penchant for stability among many intellectuals in the West reflects a certain moral fatigue. It takes strong and steady convictions to struggle every day, year after year, to uphold the principles of freedom and defend the pluralistic democratic order while maintaining the military strength to thwart aggression."[67] Moral fatigue: this was what really had to be resisted. The pursuit of stability was probably illusory. The central imperative was to restore the exercise of political will, in the interest of strategic renewal and a more secure world peace.[68]

The word *resolve* enjoyed great rhetorical prominence in the Reagan years. Indeed, it contributed again and again to the regular rallying cries for a suitably muscular and nationalist foreign policy, including a major arms build-up. In the meantime, the world was full of real, often intractable problems: problems that were messy, complex, deeply rooted, and usually resistant to simple solutions. Such problems put a premium on substantive policy-making, but this was not the forte of Reagan's Washington, particularly before 1987. The president and his followers basked in a rhetoric of simplification: a rhetoric of moral clarity, comforting answers, and happy endings. This rhetoric conformed to a vision of the world that most people *wished* to be true. Whether or not it *was* true did not concern most ordinary Americans all that much, given that there were no startling developments (that is, no really bad news) that commanded media attention and forced average citizens to pause for much serious thought. Their president's voice was appreciated as a voice of familiar values, of confidence and conviction, and of moral certainty. As Sidney Blumenthal, a writer for the *Washington Post*, observed in 1986, Ronald Reagan's "policies might be contradictory and counterproductive, but his mythology remains appealing." His central political appeal was "to the American dream he had had the good fortune to live."[69] Frances FitzGerald made a similar point in 1985. There was, she suggested, "an aesthetic to Reagan's world. Instead of a chaotic mess, there was a story line, a single sweeping arc of narrative that bound all events together and made sense of them."[70] And this narrative, couched in terms that were uplifting and reassuring, made sense of modern life, both abroad and at home, in a way which felt authentic. It was a story that people wanted to believe.

Reaganism was seen by some as a movement of renewal, by others as a kind of escapism. Undoubtedly, Ronald Reagan's celebration of dreams – notably the American Dream – went down well with his audience. As political scientist Benjamin Barber remarked in 1985: "The election of a Hollywood dreamer to an office so badly tainted has been a balm to the troubled American spirit. And the President has reminded Americans of the place of dreams in the American heart."[71] Reagan seemed able to rise above the gloom and unpleasantness of so much of mundane existence; and he had the capacity to create in his own mind and articulate for others a buoyant vision of what Americans could accomplish for themselves and the world – and all without much pain or inconvenience. Greatness, which was a part of America's destiny, would not, apparently, be all that difficult to attain. Robert Tucker, in an assessment of the outgoing administration's foreign policy in early 1989, pointed out that Reagan's "message was that sacrifice was unnecessary and that the nation might aspire to great ends without having to endure arduous means." "From the outset," he concluded, "the great appeal of the president's policies was that they demanded so little of the public while promising so much."[72] In a politics that suggested that "you can have it all," political substance and hard policy choices were repeatedly subordinated to the requirements of political theatre and to displays of the symbols of power.[73] This attentiveness to symbolism was one of the reasons for the priority attached to missiles, numbers of warheads, nuclear megatonnage, and other such tokens of high-tech potency, for these were considered visible expressions of the stature and credibility of the United States.

In late 1984, a scholar of international affairs, Stanley Hoffmann, observed that "what is spreading" in the United States "is a desire not to be bothered or battered by data."[74] President Reagan was the perfect exemplar of this desire. "The more one observes Reagan," wrote Elizabeth Drew in October 1986, "the more it seems that he lives in his own world, with his own set of realities."[75] What others might have thought of as "facts" concerning, say, SDI or arms control, or taxes or budget deficits, were apparently of little interest to him. As he was about to leave office in late 1988, the *New Yorker* reflected on his remarkable performance as head of state: "The line between entertainment and news has been blurred most successfully by President Reagan. Better than any rival, he has been able to describe the world as he wanted to see it – a description independent of any objective truth – and do it so winningly that his stories seemed almost real. His talent has been to live entirely in the present, one show at a time ... Clearly, his job has not been to run the government but to be himself, an entertainer: warm, solicitous, upbeat, manly, full of cheerful news."[76] Such a leader was not inclined to attend much to those depressing and constricting circumstances of modern life that had so often absorbed the energies of his immediate predecessor. And such a leader was not disposed to dwell on the perils and painful realities of the nuclear age. Instead, he turned away from them, preferring to concentrate his mind on American dreams and the vision of SDI.

During the Reagan years, the complexities of the real world were frequently ignored. Ideas were entertained about the world that were almost breathtaking in their simplicity and naïve optimism; some were far-fetched to the point of absurdity. (One of the means proposed to render nuclear weapons "impotent and obsolete" was the x-ray laser, which would be powered by a nuclear explosion!) These ideas, many of which were conveyed in story form, had widespread appeal. And yet stories that took little account of facts, including awkward facts, and that ignored realities out there, some of them disagreeable, were bound to become problematic, even if (perhaps especially if) it took a while for many people to see through them. Thus the questions arose: In political terms, what did all this weaponry add up to? What did it accomplish? How did it make the country more secure? However people might *feel* – and many of them clearly did feel better[77] – wasn't the country *in fact* just as physically exposed to attack, just as vulnerable to annihilation, as it had been a decade before? Objectively, then, weren't the fundamental conditions of existence in the nuclear age unaltered?

Certainly, there is no evidence that the United States arms build-up or its championing of nuclear weapons during the 1980s actually helped the country in any significant way to achieve any of its foreign policy objectives. Many problems – Central America, the turbulent Middle East, an increasingly powerful Japan – had no or virtually no connection to nuclear firepower in any form. In Europe and the Far East, Washington's relations with many of its allies were more brittle at the end of the decade than they had been at the beginning, when the West's dominant member, the United States, had allegedly been suffering from nuclear inferiority. The extraordinary upheavals that shook the Soviet Union from the mid-1980s were rooted largely in domestic politics and in the new leadership's acknowledgment of their country's long and sorry record of failure on many fronts; the Reagan administration's arms build-up was, at best, of marginal significance to the course of Soviet history, including the flurry of foreign policy concessions and accommodations to internationalism after 1985 (more about this in the next chapter). In the tumultuous world of international relations, the vast nuclear arsenal of the United States was largely, perhaps entirely, irrelevant to the success or failure of the nation's policies – as was the equally vast arsenal of the Soviet Union to the conduct of its policies. In fact, nuclear "strength" was revealed to be an exceptionally ineffective, generally

useless tool of foreign policy. While they were accorded much symbolic importance, nuclear weapons were of remarkably little value
in practice. In the course of the 1980s many people came to recognize
that a dedicated arms build-up ought not to be confused with a
coherent foreign policy.

And so it was that after much debate and agitation and expenditure of money, the fundamental nuclear realities of the late 1980s
were no different from what they had been ten years before. The
strategic balance was essentially unchanged. As McGeorge Bundy,
a political scientist who had been a White House adviser in the 1960s,
pointed out in his impressive 1988 study of the nuclear age, while
many new warheads were deployed during these years, many older
warheads were withdrawn (especially those intended for battlefield
use), with the result that "the overall numbers of weapons and of
megatons have not changed much on either side." Nor, he observed,
had any new deployment had "any large effect on the enduring
strategic stalemate." The changes were in the details of lethality,
and these changes counted for little in the superpower balance of
terror (though they might turn out to have a negative bearing on
arms control efforts in subsequent years). What endured was the
formidable logic of stalemate. Bundy represented the essence of the
situation succinctly: *"The governing reality of the nuclear balance is the
prospect of shared and sweeping catastrophe in any resort to nuclear warheads by either side."*[78] This was the heart of the matter: the probability
(who could say how probable?) of unspeakable and mutual devastation as a consequence of any use of nuclear weapons in any circumstances. This prospect had loomed over the world in the late
1960s; it continued to loom in the late 1970s and the late 1980s; and
it was virtually certain to persist into the foreseeable future. Here
was the more or less permanent reality of modern existence – a
reality that endured independently of the fervent wishes of experts
and non-experts alike to remake history and restore a kind of ele-
mental security that, though taken for granted not long before, had
suddenly and alarmingly vanished. Whether the politics of the
Soviet-American relationship at any given time were or were not
civil and accommodating, there was simply no escape for either
power from an existential state of military deadlock, mutual risk,
and shared exposure to calamity.

CHAPTER FOUR

Peace through Fear

To keep our neighbour pacified
We threaten him with homicide ...
...
We flourish weapons left and right
To show we do not mean to fight ...
                    Dennis Lee, "The Golden Rule," 1987[1]

One of the wisest judgments made about nuclear weapons came early in the Cold War. In the winter of 1949–50 when George Kennan was about to resign his position in the State Department, he raised, in a trenchant manner, the question of the role of nuclear weapons in American security policy. There was, he said, one crucial question: "Are we to rely upon weapons of mass destruction as an integral and vitally important component of our military strength, which we would expect to employ deliberately, immediately, and unhesitatingly in the event that we become involved in a military conflict with the Soviet Union? Or are we to retain such weapons in our national arsenal only as a deterrent to the use of similar weapons against ourselves or our allies and as a possible means of retaliation in case they are used?" There was no doubt, he thought, that *some* nuclear weapons would be retained. "The problem is: for what purpose, and against the background of what subjective attitude, are we to develop such weapons and to train our forces in their use?"[2]

If the role of weapons of mass destruction was deemed to be strictly deterrent-retaliatory, then the numbers of these weapons could be limited in accordance with this modest and limited role. The point of possessing nuclear weapons would be simply to deter nuclear use by another nuclear power. Accordingly, a large nuclear stockpile would be redundant and wasteful. If, however, the intention was, as Kennan put it, "to use weapons of mass destruction deliberately and prior to their use against us or our allies, in a future war, then our purpose is presumably to inflict maximum destruction on ... the enemy, with the least expenditure of effort ... In this case, the only limitations on the number and power of mass destruction weapons which we would wish to develop would presumably be those of ordinary military economy, such as cost, efficiency, and ease of delivery."[3] As we have seen in chapter one, it was this latter outlook that triumphed overwhelmingly, particularly after the outbreak of war in Korea, and not only in Washington, but also (though with rather more reservations) in the capitals of most of its allies. These were years of a pronounced nuclearization of what was usually represented as defence, or even security, policy. Nuclear weapons were central to the American handling of East-West relations, both militarily and politically. They were designed to deter and defend, to win on the battlefield, and to reassure as well.

AVERTING WAR

This explicit nuclear dependency not only became firmly entrenched, but also came to be credited with the prevention of major war. A massive nuclear arsenal was deployed; peace between the great powers persisted; and the latter, peace, was declared to be a product of the former, the deployment of nuclear weapons. Given that this arsenal was intended to deter the Soviet Union, and given that the Soviet Union did not violate any vital American interest during these years, the conclusion was drawn that the nuclear threat had indeed been successful in thwarting aggression (that is, nuclear deterrence worked). By this logic, the possession of nuclear weaponry was vindicated by history and consequently deserved to be properly maintained in the future. Thus were the nuclear threat and the free world's security linked together. "Since the end of World War II," asserted Robert Tucker in 1988, "the peace and security of the United States and its major allies have depended largely on the deterrent effect of nuclear weapons." In criticizing the 1986 Reykjavik meeting and the anti-nuclear sentiments it had legitimated, the former secretary of defense, James Schlesinger, stated: "Nuclear weapons remain the indispensable ingredient in Western deterrence strategy. For a generation the security of the Western world has rested on nuclear deterrence." This was thought to be especially true for the security of Europe: "the security of the European allies, from the beginning," claimed the strategic writer, Robert Osgood, "has been critically dependent on u.s. protection, which, in turn, has depended on a u.s. pledge to initiate the use of nuclear weapons against an attack that could not be withstood conventionally." NATO was, or at least had become, a decidedly nuclear-reliant alliance. As Schlesinger remarked in 1987, "Nuclear weapons provide the glue that has held the Western alliance together."[4]

Sometimes deterrence took on a life of its own and became an active and virtually independent historical force. According to the prominent journalist, Charles Krauthammer, in 1984: "Deterrence has a track record. For the entire postwar period it has maintained the peace between the two superpowers, preventing not only nuclear but conventional war as well. Under the logic of deterrence, proxy and brushfire wars are permitted, but not wars between the major powers. As a result, Europe, the central confrontation line between the two superpowers, has enjoyed the longest period of uninterrupted peace in a century." This was a standard argument in both civilian and military circles. Krauthammer conceded the obvious: that deterrence could fail. But "a system that has kept the peace for a generation" deserved respect, and its critics, he declared, are "morally obliged to come up with a better alternative. It makes no sense to reject deterrence simply because it may not be infallible; it makes sense to reject it only if it proves more dangerous than the alternatives. And a more plausible alternative has yet to be offered."[5]

This word "deterrence" was tossed around freely and often in a careless manner. Deterrence was said to have done this and to have caused or prevented that. Most military expenditures were made in its name. Even the Strategic Defense Initiative, which was first promoted as a way of transcending deterrence, was later said to be intended to enhance it. Strategists and planners were constantly recommending ways to strengthen deterrence; indeed, almost every new nuclear weapons system or force multiplier was justified by reference to its alleged value for deterrence. And yet the meaning of deterrence was never clear. Some people understood it to mean what others would definitely not have understood it to mean. The various meanings attached to the word pulled in different, even contrary, directions. In part because of its heavily psychological colouring (one superpower was construed to be trying to influence "the mind" of the other superpower), the notion of deterrence was inherently pliable, imprecise, and easily stretched. This one common noun was made to cover a tremendous range of conceptual territory. It was applied to diverse historical and political circumstances; it appeared repeatedly in theoretical and strategic discourse; and it seemed to cut across some of the usual divisions of political ideology. Everybody seemed to make use of the word, though frequently with radically different meanings in mind. In wrestling with this confusion, it is best, I think, to keep the word "deterrence" at arm's length and instead to speak mostly of a more concrete reality, the nuclear threat. By its very nature and existence, the weaponry after Hiroshima was a mortal threat without precedent. What concerns us is this: How did this extraordinary threat affect the conduct of superpower politics, including the planning for and aversion to war? And what conclusions can be drawn from the fact that, during the first few decades after it came to exist, the threat to use nuclear weapons, whether implicit or explicit, was never carried out? The following reflections touch briefly on these questions.

First of all, nuclear weapons undoubtedly added to the horror of war, and in so doing they may well have made peace especially attractive.[6] This view would seem to accord with common sense. Surely, it has been argued, the presence of nuclear weaponry induced statesmen and their military advisers to act with particular caution, to avoid immoderate risks, and to think much more than twice about challenging the vital interests of another great power. Given the lethality of modern arsenals, according to this argument, both superpowers and their leading allies took special pains to avoid the kind of direct East-West confrontation that might have led to armed conflict. This is certainly a plausible reading of history. Herbert York, a weapons scientist of long experience and thoughtful views, presented a balanced statement of this position in 1987: "I do not believe the claim that if it had not been for the presence of the bomb, the Soviets would have invaded Western Europe. But this last half-century has seen many small crises in Europe and elsewhere, one or more of which could have led to general war if the existence of the bomb had not greatly dampened ambitions and inclinations toward adventurism. For better and for worse, the bomb has thrown a blanket of stability over many a tinderbox that in the prenuclear world might well have burst into full flame." He spoke of the "obvious respect for and fear of the bomb" on the part of the nations of Europe – the kind of respect and fear that made all sane leaders exceptionally trigger-shy.[7]

However, it should be recognized as well that the horror of modern war might have been fully inhibiting to "adventurism," even had nuclear weapons not existed. After all, World War II, with its 55 million dead, widespread devastation, and countless savageries, had been from the perspective of most of the combatants decidedly horrible enough; and it is not self-evident that new terrors were needed to highlight the desirability of preserving the post-1945 peace. It is entirely possible (perhaps probable) that the prospect of a non-nuclear third world war would have fostered unprecedented prudence and restraint and powerfully deterred further overt aggression by any large power, including Stalin's USSR, which had no good reason seriously to risk, much less yearn for, more warfare, given what it had suffered between 1941 and 1945 and given the pressing task of consolidating the Soviet Union's power in its enlarged and for the most part unwelcoming postwar sphere of influence. Even had there been no atomic bomb, it is hard to see why any rational Soviet leadership would have invaded Western Europe, thereby triggering the sort of renewed conflagration that was hardly likely to promote the interest of either international communism or the Soviet state.

Perhaps the nuclear threat played a major role in deterring war, perhaps it did not: the fact is, we do not know and will never know. The fear of nuclear catastrophe probably did impose some restraint on the actions of the superpowers, but how would it be possible to establish the relative importance of this restraining fear? How could it be shown that this particular restraint was more important than others, much less that it was all-important? Because the non-occurrence of something over a period of years (in this case, war between the superpowers) is almost certainly due to a variety of circumstances, how can it be demonstrated that only one of these possible causes (in this case, the nuclear threat) was crucial to that non-occurrence? To say with confidence that nuclear weapons were effective as a deterrent for the West, we would have to know that the Soviet Union would have attacked, had it not been for the nuclear threat from the United States. This we do not know. Nor can we assert that nuclear weapons were irrelevant to the prevention of war, for that would require proof that Moscow would not have attacked even if there had been no threat of American *nuclear* retaliation (there certainly would have been other kinds of retaliatory threats), and this again we will never know.[8] The proposition that nuclear deterrence kept the peace is not a matter of knowledge, it is a matter of belief and often rather dogmatic belief. Sceptics have suggested that it would be more becoming for the believers to refrain from complacency, given what is at risk if the system were ever to break down. One breakdown would alter the track record, in the believers' own terms, from perfect to zero.

While it is often said that nuclear weapons have served both United States interests and the interest of peace – indeed, the two have been seen as more or less identical – one is struck by the remarkable weakness of the arguments supporting these claims. In fact, it seems that the bomb was a rather poor persuader, even during those years when overwhelming predominance in nuclear firepower belonged to Washington. In the years immediately after 1945, Stalin achieved most of what he wanted to achieve in eastern Europe and effectively imposed his will through force (save in Yugoslavia), despite the lack of an atomic arsenal. The historian, Adam Ulam, remarked in the mid-1970s that "in retrospect one may venture to say that the era of the American monopoly of the atom bomb passed without any special advantage accruing to the United States on its account,"[9] and later research has mostly confirmed this judgment. If anything is to be particularly credited for the apparent success of the American policy of containment, it is the Marshall Plan and its billions of dollars of aid for a ravaged Europe, not the existence of American weapons of mass destruction. In the 1950s and early 1960s, when the Soviet Union had some nuclear weapons but the Americans had many more, this American superiority seems to have had little bearing on the successful prosecution of Washington's foreign policy. It is certainly possible that one or two of the several United States threats to use the bomb during these years may have given the other side cause to act more cautiously, but the evidence is very incomplete and perhaps will remain so. However, the most compelling conclusion to emerge thus far is this: there is, as yet, not a single well-documented instance of the United States nuclear threat clearly either preventing war, or bringing peace, or protecting a vital American interest.[10]

There was, in fact, a major discrepancy between, on the one hand, the confident assertion that American nuclear weapons kept the peace or at least played a vital role in keeping the peace and, on the other hand, the thinness of the evidence offered in support of this assertion. Much of this evidence was slight and often circumstantial; and numerous historians have presented plausible explanations for war avoidance during times of tension, or for peace creation at the conclusion of conflicts, which attributed little influence to the threatened use of nuclear weapons. The orthodox claims for the political-strategic utility of nuclear weapons were very much stronger than the facts would warrant. The role of the bomb in terminating the war against Japan in 1945 and in saving the lives of American soldiers, for example, was greatly exaggerated, because it was almost certain that the Japanese would have surrendered before any United States land invasion, especially in light of the Soviet declaration of war on 8 August, which clearly sealed Japan's fate.[11] Similarly, it is by no means clear that President Eisenhower's nuclear threats in the spring of 1953 carried particular weight in the termination of war in Korea that summer; other factors seem to have been more important in furthering the peace process, notably the death of Stalin in March 1953 and the more flexible and accommodating policies of the new Soviet leadership. While it cannot be said that Washington's signals of possible nuclear use had no influence on the settlement of this war, there is certainly no evidence that these threats were of central importance, and there is a persuasive case to be made that they were, at best, of secondary significance.[12]

While it is possible, then, that the mere presence of nuclear weapons at times of major Cold War crises, such as the Cuban missile crisis, heightened the fear of escalation and thus encouraged prudent statecraft, it cannot be said that these weapons were of much direct political value to their possessors. Nuclear threats, either to coerce or to deter, were certainly not nearly as politically constructive as many American officials and nuclear theorists thought they were. These insiders tended to have a vested interest in having others believe and in believing themselves in the crucial importance of what they spoke of as America's nuclear strength. After all, these men were the architects, promoters, and rationalizers of their nation's nuclear dependency and thus were not likely to be especially attentive to or appreciative of arguments and evidence that cast doubt on the merits of this dependency. Given the conventional wisdom that the nuclear deterrent was vital to United States security, it is not particularly surprising that historical explanations were regularly set forth to justify this orthodoxy. Thus the satisfactory outcomes – or, more accurately, the non-disastrous outcomes – of various East-West disputes were repeatedly credited to the deterrent, whatever the specifics of the situation and the alternative readings of the evidence. Those responsible, politically and professionally, for the nuclear build-up and its elaborate infrastructure had reason to simplify complex political realities and to see the history of the Cold War from a particular and strongly biased angle of vision. Hence, in part, their recurrent and far from impartial declarations that deterrence had worked and was still working. Other plausible explanations for the persistence of peace were largely ignored.

Moreover, even if one grants that the United States nuclear arsenal may have exerted a restraining influence on the Kremlin, there is no doubt that this formidable arsenal and the prominence Americans attached to it gave Moscow the strongest possible incentive to build its own nuclear arsenal so as to correct the problem, from its point of view, of American invulnerability. (It would appear, as well, that it was American threats of nuclear use in Asia in the 1950s that stimulated the development of nuclear weapons by China.)[13] If the atomic bomb was, according to some Western strategists, a godsend for postwar America and a welcome way of offsetting the power of the Red Army,[14] it also marked the end of American security and the initiation of the United States into the international club of vulnerable nations. And whereas this latter development was undeniable, the former claim – that the bomb was a winning or at least an equalizing weapon – was not. Indeed, claims for the bomb's utility have always been contested and very difficult to prove. Nuclear weaponry may or may not have prevented a third world war, but there is no doubt at all about the effect on United States security once the Soviet Union also acquired the capacity to threaten virtually limitless destruction.

If deterrence was, as so often was claimed, the basis of Western security, it was also a policy with distinct limitations. Nuclear deterrence was an *overwhelmingly negative* policy: it highlighted threats and punitive sanctions and ignored or deprecated the value of positive inducements. Deterrence is inherently retributive, not creative. This emphatic negativism undermined the search for security by other paths, notably those approaches that stressed the value of diplomacy, negotiated agreements, and collaboration based on mutual interests. The preoccupation with deterrent threats tended to foreclose discussion about the handling of East-West relations and to downgrade or exclude from consideration other ways of dealing with the Soviet Union. Another negative aspect of deterrence arose from its heavy emphasis on displays of resolve. Firmness and standing tall could so easily become intransigence and bellicosity. Tough posturing by one side, in the name of deterrence, frequently elicited similar resolute posturing by the other side, with a consequent increase in tensions between them. Deterrence doctrine also led to an excessive fixation on the prospect of aggression to the exclusion of other potential causes of war, such as failures in crisis management, regional disputes that might suck the great powers in against their wills, and the destabilizing impact of nuclear threats themselves.[15] The apparent rationality of deterrence theory made little allowance for the tragic dimension of human experience: those tragedies that are liable to result from miscalculation, or bungling, or panic and confusion, or hasty and ill-considered action under pressure. It is probable that fear of aggression and clumsy efforts to forestall a feared aggression are more likely to cause war (as they have so often caused war in the past) than is aggression itself.[16]

Another limitation of deterrence as a policy lies in the fact that with nuclear threats, as with other threats, the view of the prospective victim differs from that of the prospective victimizer. What are salutary and strictly restraining threats to the side that sees itself as deterring (as each side does) are liable to be interpreted by those against whom the threats are directed as dangerously hostile. While each nuclear power is inclined to think largely or entirely in terms of its own retaliatory capacity, the nation that is targeted by these weapons is more likely to contemplate their offensive, possibly first-strike, implications. (Such contrasting perceptions seem to have existed at the time of the Cuban missile crisis.)[17] Deterrence became a kind of buzz word; but what it was taken to mean by those who

spoke of it depended fundamentally on whether the speaker identified himself with the potential victim or the proud possessor of
nuclear weapons. What was novel about the nuclear age was that
the two superpowers became, potentially, *both* victims and victimizers, perhaps even simultaneously victims and victimizers.

As I have noted, the insistence on deterrent threats as the foundation of peace tended to crowd out and suppress diplomatic approaches to East-West relations and, in so doing, made it more likely
that those opportunities for reducing tensions that did arise were
not followed up. Such missed opportunities were partly a consequence of the excessively weapons-centred conception of the rivalry
between the superpowers – a rivalry that need not have been as
obsessively absorbed with matters of lethal hardware and overkill
as it actually was. When political energies were being invested heavily in weapons build-ups, other and less threatening initiatives –
initiatives designed to accommodate differences and reinforce mutual interests – were liable to be inadequately supported and thus
not come to very much.

The later 1950s was such a time of missed opportunities. The
pertinent circumstances of these Khrushchev-Eisenhower years
have been well summarized in *Russia: The Roots of Confrontation*, a
book by the American historian, Robert Daniels, that is generally
critical of the history of the Soviet revolution. Nikita Khrushchev,
Daniels thinks,

actually went an extraordinary distance in 1956–1959 to extend the olive
branch of arms limitation to the West. He offered concessions in the very
areas that Stalin had been most rigid about – namely, inspection and conventional force reductions. U.S. leaders at the time, as well as many subsequent commentators, have dismissed these Soviet proposals as
propaganda gestures. The fact remains that during these years the Soviets
took unusual initiatives in foreign policy and in domestic affairs, in distinct
contrast to their practice both before and after. It is unlikely that any Soviet
leader would take such steps as Khrushchev did (even including unilateral
troop reductions and the 1958 test moratorium) for purely propaganda reasons. However, the Khrushchev initiatives, whatever their value, were not
capitalized on by the United States and its allies; Soviet party and military
leaders must have viewed them as a failure of monumental proportions.
By increasing Khrushchev's vulnerability to the neo-Stalinist opposition in
the party, the West's rebuff no doubt weakened him politically and contributed to his 1960 switch to a hard line in an effort to recoup.[18]

Partial confirmation of Daniels's view is to be found in the recollections of a Soviet defector, Arkady Shevchenko, a former official

in the Soviet foreign ministry. Despite a generally unsympathetic view of Soviet politics in his book, *Breaking With Moscow*, Shevchenko recalled his feelings about Khrushchev's objectives in the later 1950s: "I believed that Khrushchev was making a genuine effort to reach an accord with the United States and other Western countries on at least some measures for limiting the arms race, and that he was moving our country in the right direction." Some Canadian officials at the time were similarly persuaded that Moscow was genuinely seeking some sort of settlement with the West, particularly with regard to the arms race.[19] Shevchenko remembered feeling "convinced that the Soviet Union was more interested in real progress than the United States was." A superior told him "that Khrushchev was very bitter about the United States' position and that of its allies."[20]

This American reluctance to respond to Soviet initiatives during the later 1950s has been fairly well established. As one American scholar, Matthew Evangelista, observed: "U.S. officials at the time seemed willing to pocket Soviet concessions without giving anything in return, while at the same time playing down the significance of the unilateral reductions in the USSR's armed forces."[21] Agreements to reduce or constrain armaments were simply not a high priority for the Eisenhower administration. No doubt there were various reasons for this unresponsive American position, but surely one of the most important was that Washington had already committed itself to a massive nuclear build-up, a major "strengthening of the U.S. deterrent," and many people had a vested interest in ensuring that this build-up not be curtailed in any way. During the last three years of Eisenhower's presidency the American nuclear arsenal more than tripled, from less than 6,000 warheads to something in excess of 18,000 warheads.[22] Given such investments and priorities, the tepid United States response to the thaw in Moscow is, in retrospect, not so hard to understand.

Deterrence not only injected an excessive negativism into the conduct of foreign policy in the 1950s, but it also soon came to be regarded as insufficient in itself as a basis for peace over the long term. Even some of the leading advocates of the "great deterrent" acknowledged on occasion that the stability provided by the deterrent might be only temporary. Thus Sir John Slessor admitted in 1956: "No one can pretend that this truce of terror is a comfortable state of affairs in which to live, and we should never come to regard it as anything but a temporary condition to be terminated just as soon as a practical alternative presents itself ... There is no argument that the present situation is safe; the only question is whether there is any immediate prospect of a safer situation."[23] The possible impermanence of deterrence gave pause for thought and for doubts. As a book published in 1956 by the Council of Foreign Relations, *Russia and America: Dangers and Prospects*, put it: "It is hard to believe that real and lasting stability is to be found in an endless piling up of thermonuclear weapons and means of delivery among an everincreasing number of nations. One cannot but have the uneasy feeling that sooner or later something may go wrong and lead to the physical destruction of our civilization."[24] In the view of numerous thoughtful observers, there was (perhaps) a kind of safety through mutual terror, but it was a perverse sort of safety and the peace that it seemed to have induced could not necessarily be counted on to last, at least not without other, more positive political reinforcements. The question kept coming up: Was time really on the side of a strategy of peace through fear? Herbert York, sensitive to the tension between the possibly deterrent-based peace of the moment and the requirements for long-term survival, has commented: "Maybe, just maybe, we can count on that situation [mutual deterrence] to persist *until* the time when we can achieve a real and permanent solution."[25]

That nuclear threats are not enough has always been appreciated in some circles. Peace, it was believed, was not likely to be sustainable only or largely out of fear of nuclear attack. The political scientist, Joseph Nye, said of deterrence: "Even as it buys time while we look for alternatives, it is important to reduce reliance on deterrence in the long term. We need to look at processes of influence, accommodation, and cooperation that can reduce the acuteness of the security dilemma."[26] Perhaps the nuclear threat, as an existential fact of life, would last for a very long time; but this threat would have to be combined with other, more positive levers and with less frightening modes of political exchange. McGeorge Bundy put this case well: "I propose that deterrence, however it works, should always be considered in the context of two other interconnected objectives – reassurance of friends and détente with adversaries. Deterrence is part, but only part, of the politics of nations."[27] And it can only be a part principally for one reason: fear and terror, the essence of the nuclear deterrent threat, are unable on their own to provide the basis for avoiding nuclear catastrophe. When a crisis erupts, frightened adversaries are likely to be very dangerous adversaries. Fervent proponents of deterrence have been and are insufficiently attentive to the corrosive – and explosive – power of fear.

Finally, and on a more optimistic note, the fact of nuclear non-use since 1945 has fostered a tradition of non-use and in consequence the risk of nuclear war may well have diminished. Traditions tend to become encrusted; the longer they last the more difficult they are to overturn. The many years in which nuclear weapons existed but were not used have provided a formidable array of pressures against breaking this tradition – a tradition that almost all attentive citizens in all countries wish to see continue. This tradition has been a major constraint on trigger-happy ideologues and militarists. War-charged situations in the past, most of them in the first two decades of the Cold War, did not result in war between the superpowers, and the longer this avoidance of war lasted the better things were bound to become (because tension cannot usually be sustained in peacetime at a high level indefinitely) and the better they did in fact become – better in the sense that time served as a healer and allowed for an enlarged political commitment in both East and West to processes of conciliation, accommodation, and confidence-building. This generalization has been true despite certain setbacks, such as those of the early 1980s. Over the four decades since the late 1940s, the risk of catastrophic war has probably been reduced; and these risks can continue to be reduced in the future through wise and sensible political action.

Armageddon, then, though an inescapable possibility, is not (as some people fear) virtually inevitable. McGeorge Bundy has put the case for not becoming desperate: "Reduction of the risk, decade by decade, is our best hope for long-run survival. It is a mathematical law that if you do not reduce the risk from one time period to the next, you face inevitable catastrophe, but it is also a mathematical law that if you keep reducing the risk, your chance of durable safety can be very good. Thus if the overall chance of general nuclear disaster *per decade* was one in fifty in the decade of the sixties (when most of the danger was in one week of 1962), and if it is one in two hundred two decades later, if we can make it one in eight hundred for the first decade of the twenty-first century, and so on after that, the chance of permanent escape will be 99 percent." Of course, as Bundy realized, such "mathematics of probability do not of themselves produce safety." Safety, or at least diminished insecurity, will depend on sound choices and political judgments in the future. Mutual interests can be cultivated; common concerns can build political bridges; habits of distrust and hostility can be eroded and perhaps eventually cast aside. "In the long run," Bundy observes, "only mutual trust, not arms control as such, can end any military rivalry."[28] And if such trust can be forged, it will be a product in part of a shared acknowledgment by the great powers of the obsolescence of war as an instrument of state policy.

PREPARING FOR WAR

During the 1950s, the Soviet authorities spoke repeatedly of American "preparations for atomic war." These claims were largely propaganda; they conveniently ignored Moscow's own formidable non-nuclear forces and its coercive use of this power; and it was hard not to notice that these Soviet complaints became less frequent once the Kremlin had gained the capacity to make credible nuclear threats of its own. However, as we saw in chapter one, these charges of United States preparations for a nuclear war were not entirely inaccurate. For even as Washington was hoping to avoid such a war, it was also preparing to fight one. It had plans to initiate the use of nuclear weapons and, "if necessary," to fight a nuclear war to a "successful conclusion"; or, as an alternative strategic formulation put it, Washington wanted to be able to terminate a nuclear war on terms "favourable" to the United States. These were strategic commitments that embraced a traditional approach to war, notably the idea that victory was still in some sense a meaningful concept. Accordingly, the possession of all kinds of destructive force, including nuclear force, was potentially useful. In certain respects nuclear weapons could be used in the same manner as conventional ones, and when possessed in abundance, these modern instruments of warfare could be effectively deployed to enhance the nation's security.

These traditional military doctrines were prevalent among planners and theorists in the 1950s and, though not much publicized, they remained so three decades later. In 1988, the chief of staff of the USAF, General Larry D. Welch, wrote in a foreword to an air force publication of "our fundamental purpose as a Service," which he said was "to deter war, but to be prepared to fight and win should deterrence fail."[29] This formulation plays down the significance of the nuclear revolution and conceives of war in traditional terms. Speaking in 1987 of America's "nuclear commanders," Russell E. Dougherty, a retired general who had once been one of them, thought that "the morality of war, even nuclear war, is just not an issue with them: they are American warriors at the zenith of their profession. Fighting wars, with the equipment and weapons issued them, is their job."[30]

There was no doubt among strategists that nuclear weapons could be used to punish and thus (they hoped) to deter attack through the threat of retaliation; but beyond this self-evident fact of life they made the further claim that deterrence required a credible nuclear war-fighting capability and that any proper military strategy had to be concerned with how to act if deterrence failed (always a possibility) and consequently warfare, probably nuclear warfare, "had to be" conducted. "If we cannot win," wrote a senior air force military scientist in the 1960s, "we cannot deter." He spoke of expenditures "to strengthen SAC's war-fighting, therefore deterrent, capability."[31] Believing in the continuing political relevance of war, these strategists were naturally concerned with actual scenarios for fighting a war. Thus, for example, the authors of a 1984 book on the Trident nuclear-armed submarine concluded their laudatory account with the following statement: "Defense analysts in and out of government must ... succeed in thinking more profoundly and sensibly than they did during the era of détente, with its self-delusory vocabulary. Strategic parity, essential equivalence, graduated response, mutual assured destruction, [strategic arms negotiations], and mutual assured vulnerability never can serve as alternatives to the ability to conduct war, when necessary, in the national defense. Fortunately, Trident can fight as well as deter."[32]

To strategists still attached to this warrior tradition, the nuclear battlefield could be rendered advantageous to the United States. In the view of one government official, employed with the Nuclear Command and Control System Support Staff and writing in 1989 in support of the utility of nuclear artillery and the need to improve it: "The most fundamental point about the deterrent role of AFAPS [artillery-fired atomic projectiles] is not the number of weapons lost [in a war in Europe against the Warsaw pact], but rather the number that survives to influence Soviet deterrent calculations. If only a handful of AFAPS survived, they could still perform their deterrent and escalation control functions. The execution of even a few AFAPS would thwart Pact combat operations and signal NATO's resolve to defend its interests. By raising the specter of escalation, AFAPS can link NATO's defense to U.S. strategic nuclear forces and encourage the prompt cessation of hostilities."[33] This was a vision of a nuclear battlefield that functioned in much the same way as ideal battlefields had always functioned: that is, as a theatre in which lethal force, now including tactical nuclear forces, could be applied and perhaps would be applied in a limited, selective, and disciplined manner. Soviet officialdom may have included a few military men who shared these views, though in general Moscow was much less attached than Washington to doctrines of controlled nuclear use.[34]

By the mid-1950s, nuclear weaponry was being treated as the primary currency of power in world politics. Various sovereign states, including Sweden, thought seriously about acquiring this power (and a few actually did so); and the military establishments

of the great, once great, and hoping-to-be-great powers became reluctant to make do with pre-nuclear firepower when the new weaponry that science had created was so much more efficiently
destructive. If nuclear weaponry really was the wave of the future,
as the United States emphasis on both massive retaliation and tactical
nuclear war-fighting strongly implied and as the hefty budgetary
support for Strategic Air Command, the nation's foremost nuclear
fist in the 1950s and 1960s, confirmed, then it seemed clear to the
military services in the West that they had better learn to ride this
wave and thereby get a piece of the nuclear action. In the United
States, institutional self-preservation in all three services became
closely linked to the acquisition of a range of nuclear capabilities. It
was not long before the war plans of these services included detailed
scenarios for the use of nuclear weapons, whether in sea battles,
land battles, air bombardment, "strategic exchanges," or attempts
to thwart a nuclear attack with "defensive" nuclear weapons. One
assumes that the authorities in Moscow and Beijing, when developing their own nuclear arsenals, drew certain lessons from the
example of the ambitious and wide-ranging war plans of the world's
leading nuclear power.

Such planning for the use of nuclear weapons, covering a wide
variety of conflict situations, was central to the military view of
deterrence, which usually resisted a merely retaliatory posture. Deterrence was taken to include war-fighting strategies, some of them
remarkably ambitious. Thus, for example, Zbigniew Brzezinski, the
national security adviser to President Carter, recorded that with the
approval of a new presidential directive in November 1979, "for the
first time the United States deliberately sought for itself the capability
to manage a protracted nuclear conflict,"[35] a capability that was
pursued even more strenuously by the next administration. This
was only one of many testimonials to the technocratic and mana-
gerial assumptions that underlay Washington's approach to what
George Kennan had regarded as weaponry of little political utility,
but which many others treated as a critical instrument of foreign
policy. In 1962 the distinguished student of politics, Hans Morgenthau, spoke of the "impossibility of adapting nuclear violence to the
limited objectives of foreign policy"[36]: the point to emphasize, however, is that this view was never endorsed by the military. In fact,
it was committed to the opposite proposition – the proposition that
it *is* possible to harness nuclear violence to the goals of state policy.

In the later 1980s, one of the best publicized expressions of this
commitment to sophisticated war preparations was the doctrine of
"discriminate deterrence," a set of beliefs that was endorsed in early

1988 in a special report to the secretary of defense by the Commission on Integrated Long-Term Strategy, co-chaired by Fred C. Iklé and Albert Wohlstetter.[37] Brzezinski, who had remained a major voice in United States security debates and was a member of this commission, was one of the champions of the new opportunities that were said to be emerging as a result of improved technology. In a 1988 article in *Foreign Affairs*, he declared that "technological refinements have ... given rise to altogether novel opportunities for far more selective and strictly military uses of nuclear weaponry." He called for the full exploitation of these alleged selective capabilities of nuclear force; this was the path that ought to be followed to enhance deterrence and respond to a wide range of security threats. "On the strategic level it must be recognized that technological changes have wrought a revolution in the way nuclear weapons may be used in the future. They are no longer just crude instruments for inflicting massive societal devastation but can be used with precision for more specific military missions, with relatively limited collateral societal damage. The increased versatility of nuclear weapons is the consequence of the interaction between smaller warheads and highly accurate delivery systems. The result is that nuclear weapons are no longer primarily blunt instruments of deterrence but can also serve as potentially decisive instruments of discriminating violence."[38] In other words, nuclear weapons could be made useful and usable, like all weapons before them.

This view was yet another example of the relentless optimism that had long pervaded so much American thinking about nuclear weapons. This confidence in the political worth of advanced military technology – technology that, it was assumed, could be wisely managed and creatively deployed – was almost a constant in the United States approach to national security in the postwar decades. Brzezinski assumed that technological innovation could be turned to the nation's advantage as long as its citizens made the necessary effort. He was keen to rally support for the cause: "the United States in the years ahead must take advantage of its enormous capacity for technological innovation to enhance its military flexibility. Over the last several decades," he lamented, "the United States has gradually become a military Gulliver, enormously powerful yet clumsy and inert." A strategic rejuvenation was both necessary and possible. And while high technology was not a cure-all, "it does provide the basis for effective and rapid coordination, for precision in operations, for enhanced intelligence and for prompt concentration of destructive power. America is almost uniquely equipped to exploit these technological capabilities."[39] To prevent war, the United States had to possess a credible capacity to fight a war, whether nuclear or non-nuclear; and in preparing for war, it had to acquire and maintain a clear superiority in military technology.

Preparations for war were also said to convey the right messages to foreigners: messages of firmness and determination, of muscular self-confidence, and of a leadership that would have no truck with any policy that smacked of appeasement. Other nations had to be convinced of American power and of American willingness (not just capacity) to use this power; thus evidence of preparedness for war was justified as a means of highlighting this willingness and enhancing the credibility of the nuclear threat. Technological self-restraint might be interpreted as weakness and irresolution. And that could offer an inducement to Soviet aggression. Here, then, was the old refrain: peace through strength. As a 1960 editorial in the journal *Orbis* had put it: "Soviet belief in our capabilities will be in proportion to the scale, diversification and deployment of our weapons systems." And Moscow had to be pressed to believe as well "in our determination to use nuclear weapons."[40] Such thinking, which was entirely commonplace then and perhaps only slightly less so in the 1980s, was so open-ended in its implications that it amounted to a virtual blank cheque for weapons without limit.

The weapons makers themselves were an important constituency in this system of war preparation and they needed little in the way of military doctrine or deterrence theory to fuel their endeavours. They had been given a lot of money to spend, and they had technical challenges to meet and profitable operations to keep going, whether scientific or industrial. They were important parts of a largely self-sustaining system of continuing weapons production. Solly Zuckerman, the chief scientific adviser to Britain's minister of defence between 1960 and 1971, recalled in his memoirs the opposition from the weapons makers to the attempts of the late 1950s to ban nuclear testing, and added: "With all but limitless resources at their disposal, the American weapons laboratories were designing new varieties of nuclear weapons without waiting to ask how they were going to be used."[41] If a new weapon were shown to be technically feasible, the odds were that it would be built, regardless of its long-term implications for national security, which were frequently negative and counterproductive. This was what happened with the MIRV technology. The decision to place several warheads (which could be independently targeted) on a single missile was initiated by the United States in the late 1960s, but in due course there was much alarm in Washington when the Soviet Union's heavy ICBMs were modernized with MIRVs from the mid-1970s. A similar process was anticipated in the late 1980s with regard to sea-launched cruise missiles (SLCMs), which were then an American advantage; for it was predicted that if and when Moscow were to follow this American lead and deploy hundreds of its own long-range SLCMs, the United States would be the long-term loser because it is much more vulnerable to maritime attack than the USSR.

Military officials and scientists have always had a vested interest in creating whatever could be created and in steadily spinning out new ideas for military hardware. As one of them remarked in September 1989: "There's a lot to be said for following the technology and seeing where it leads, rather than agreeing in advance where you have to stop."[42] Self-restraint was considered to be both bureaucratically and scientifically unprofitable. All sorts of military technologies were pursued as long as they were judged to be in some sense technically promising, and the political implications of these innovations and refinements were rarely thought through very carefully. The military hardware that could be created was, by and large, actually produced and deployed. Yet it often made for long-term instabilities, heightened fears, and enlarged insecurities. As others acquired them, the initial possessors of advanced weapons almost always became potential victims of these weapons as well.

Let us conclude this discussion of war preparation with three further observations.

First, in the decades after World War II future weapons development was increasingly rooted, not in perceived current requirements, but in imagined requirements for ten or fifteen years into the future. Decisions taken at any given time – to approve or initiate a new weapons programme – were more and more reactions to developments that might possibly occur a good many years down the road. Planners imagined what the other side might do in the rather distant future. However, because there was no way of knowing what might happen politically in ten or fifteen years, they tended to work from the conservative assumption that little would change – thus, they imagined particular future actions of a threatening nature by the other side (deployments of new weapons) that would require appropriate reactions by their side (also deployments of new weapons). In other words, new weapons systems were justified not by reference to what a rival had done or was doing but by reference to what it was conceived that rival might do in a particular future which might very well not come to pass. Thus the weapons producers laboured to satisfy requirements that they themselves had created. Whether or not such supposed requirements would ever actually exist was a different matter. In fact, the "threats" that the new weapons were designed to address might well turn out to be largely imaginary and not worth counteracting.

The logic of this process reminds us that weapons development went on remarkably independently. It was largely unaffected by political changes, such as a relaxation of Cold War tensions or a partial resolution of political differences. The authors of an admirable guide to the nuclear system, *Nuclear Battlefields: Global Links in the Arms Race*, emphasized this often unrecognized fact of modern political life: "Whether it be the height of 'detente' or the height of East-West hostility, at any given moment the collection of 'intelligence' continues, the airwaves stay filled with messages, forces maneuver, weapons get developed and tested, and the missiles, submarines, and bombers stand ready for instant action, oblivious to the world around them. These activities guarantee that the other side will do at least the same; each side uses them as evidence that the other side is planning and preparing for the worst." As they aptly observed: "Occasionally, when u.s. and Soviet ships collide, or planes get shot down, we are reminded that something is going on out there that seems to have a life of its own."[43] Military science marched mostly to its own tune. Military technologies, including those related to nuclear weapons and their delivery systems, had become disengaged from public policy and what is sometimes spoken of as grand strategy. And this disengagement grew increasingly acute as the lethal technologies at issue became ever more elaborate, exotic, and arcane.

Second, the nuclear age put the military establishments of the superpowers in a potentially (some would say inescapably) untenable position with respect to preparedness for war. On the one hand, like all armed forces in history, they saw their role to be to fight with whatever weapons were available to win wars for the political ends decided upon by their nations' governments. On the other hand, there was a widespread opinion both inside and outside the various relevant political élites that actually to fight a war with nuclear weapons might be – indeed, probably would be – suicidal. The superpowers' armed forces thus planned to do something that, understandably, they had no clear idea how to do: to fight a war with nuclear weapons that would not be suicidal. It was hard to imagine that the result of any such war would be anything other than unspeakable disaster – conceivably, with "luck," "only" an unspeakable disaster for, say, the Germans or the Middle East.

The consequence of this absurd situation was that these war-fighting scenarios soon became detached from standards of assessment that most people would have associated with tolerable reality.

And yet this devising of scenarios continued to flourish. One insider, a retired official with long service in the United States Air Force, revealed the inherent contradictions in nuclear strategy, perhaps unintentionally, in a remark of 1989. He pointed out that, to defence strategists, deterrence required that "we must have the requisite forces to mete out punishment, a doctrine and strategy for employment of these forces, and the expressed political will to fight. To the military this means a battle-plan, and plans make no sense unless one has a strategy to prevail. For the military professional, there is no deterrence without a strategy to win, even if 'winning' in the nuclear context may be a grotesque abstraction."[44] The planning to prevail, then, which was thought to be essential, was also acknowledged to be radically out of touch with what experience and imagination and common sense suggested would be the almost certain chaos and human catastrophe, should such plans ever start to be executed.

Third, although the war plans of the nuclear age had potential consequences that were almost unimaginably cataclysmic, these plans and the mechanisms to put them into effect were largely hidden from public view. A lot was kept secret; information was withheld and concealed; and public discussion of nuclear issues was actively discouraged. This pervasive secrecy, commonplace since the beginning of the nuclear age, was remarked on in the mid-1950s by Richard Stebbins in his 1953 volume for the Council on Foreign Relations: "What was clear was that national policies of decisive importance to every citizen were now being framed on the basis of military and scientific calculations over which the citizen had no control and which even his elected representatives had to accept largely on faith. Even the substance of policy was likely to be conveyed in the form of condensed slogans which sounded impressive in the abstract but whose application to real situations was not always easy to visualize."[45] Writing some years later, in 1962, Hans Morgenthau thought that the Atomic Energy Commission, the body then especially responsible for developing new nuclear weapons, "has become a kind of state within the state": "A few years ago, a very high official of our government told me that the Atomic Energy Commission would not tell him how many nuclear weapons we had. And recently, a former high official of the Atomic Energy Commission corroborated this experience from the other side by telling me that there are lots of things the State Department ought to know nothing about and which ought to remain a matter between the President and the director of the Central Intelligence Agency. There exists, then, a special secrecy within the general secrecy of the government which serves the purpose of protecting the monopolistic position of certain technological elites, of which the elite of the nuclear scientists is the most eminent and the most influential one."[46] These élites, whether technological or strategic, civilian or military, were intent on keeping the public as ignorant as possible about the nature of their activities, thereby maximizing their own remarkably autonomous power and authority.

The passage of time revealed ever more evidence of this secrecy and concealment. People learned of nuclear weapons accidents and near accidents that had been hushed up, some of them in fact or potentially very serious; of nuclear safety standards that had been diluted or ignored; of contaminated nuclear sites that had been improperly attended to; of disinformation from military laboratories when it suited their purposes (such as doctored evidence from the Lawrence Livermore Laboratory concerning supposed SDI breakthroughs); of covert connections between France and the United States concerning nuclear weapons developments; and of probable operational plans for ICBM launch-on-warning that contradicted the stated American policy of riding out an attack before retaliating.[47] In the Soviet Union such state secrecy and concealment were even more pronounced. Whenever the cloak of secrecy was lifted, at least a little, what was learned was rarely reassuring. When the USAF revealed in 1989 the previously secret development costs of the B-2 bomber, which turned out to be some $22 billion for an aircraft of doubtful purpose that had never taxied down a runway, many congressmen were not at all pleased and began to ask tough questions.[48] As Morgenthau had said, the nuclear weapons establishment really did enjoy a charmed and privileged existence, beyond many of the normal processes of accountability. This was a closed, self-protective world, with its own mystique. An admirable book by John Simpson on "the military atom" and its role in the Anglo-American relationship, published in 1983, had been given a particularly appropriate title, for its special subject and for much more since 1945: *The Independent Nuclear State*.

This independent (or semi-independent) nuclear state was radically at odds with democratic principles. Its managers, the custodians and operators of the nuclear system, were assiduous in insisting on a high degree of autonomy for themselves and in resisting public enquiries into the exercise of their extraordinary powers. They commonly resented such scrutiny and regarded it as intrusive, unwarranted, and perhaps even unpatriotic (exposures, they suggested, might undermine national security and provide succour to the enemy). Senior military officers sometimes expressed concern that inordinate civilian freedom of enquiry might undermine the military's own freedom of action and inhibit its ability to use the weapons under its command. According to Elmo Zumwalt, Jr, a prominent retired admiral, writing on "escalatory conflict" in 1987: "The media and public opinion have become extraordinarily important factors in conflict situations that involve increasing levels of violence. We should be concerned about this issue as the Soviets attempt to harass our borders with hostile subversives and to manipulate the American free press. Freedom of the press is a wonderful thing and a great source of our national strength. There may come a time of emergency, however, when freedom *from* the press – that is, through censorship or a state secrets act – may be necessary."[49] Others, too, spoke of restricting debate and public discussion, in the interest of effective military cohesion and national unity.[50] To a degree, such views were inherent in the special outlook of military professionals, for whom peace is, in a sense, abnormal and war normal; and the conduct of war, of course, with its commitment to command and obedience and authoritarian practices, is deeply and inescapably hostile to the principles of liberal democracy. On the one hand, the United States put special emphasis on individual freedoms, human rights, and the need to limit state power; yet, on the other hand, it repeatedly highlighted its absolute power to destroy, which it called its deterrent, and represented this destructive power as a principal tool, sometimes even as *the* principal tool, in its national mission of protecting free peoples and securing liberal values. The contradictions in this position were not, for the most part, seriously addressed.

NEW THINKING

Shortly after Mikhail Gorbachev's ascent to supreme power in March 1985, the Soviet leader and his supporters began to talk a lot about their "new thinking." Gorbachev's own widely read book, *Perestroika*, published in 1987, was subtitled, *New Thinking for Our Country and the World*. In it he discussed a range of issues, including the politics of survival in the nuclear age. He emphasized the growth of global interdependence, the commonality of much of contemporary human experience, and the need for "joint solutions" to many of the world's pressing problems. In one passage, he set forth his basic outlook on the hazards of life in the late twentieth century: "Although the prospect of death in a nuclear war is undoubtedly the most appalling scenario possible, the issue is broader than that. The spiraling arms race, coupled with the military and political realities of the world and the persistent traditions of pre-nuclear political thinking, impedes cooperation between countries and peoples, which – East and West agree – is indispensable if the world's nations want to preserve nature intact, to ensure the rational use and reproduction of her resources and, consequently, to survive as befits human beings."[51]

Such sentiments would have been considered quite remarkable had they come from almost any Western leader in the mid-1980s; to hear them expressed by the leader of the Soviet Union took almost everyone by surprise. Nobody had ever before heard a Soviet leader speak of world affairs in this strikingly open-minded and undogmatic manner, and apparently speak in all seriousness and not just for propaganda effect. In fact, in the late 1980s it became increasingly clear that Gorbachev meant what he said and was genuinely striving to match words with appropriate actions: thus, for example, his unilateral arms reductions and nuclear test moratorium, the acceptance of on-site procedures for treaty verification, the withdrawal of Soviet military forces from Afghanistan, a much more hands-off policy toward Eastern Europe, and expanded Soviet support for the efforts of the United Nations. All of this was extraordinary and substantially without precedent, and it happened quickly and to a large extent without warning. The traditional terms of political discourse in East-West relations were suddenly outdated and out of tune with the way the world was moving. All sorts of assumptions were subjected to intensified scrutiny, among them the role of nuclear weapons in the pursuit and preservation of national security and international peace.

There were four key elements in Gorbachev's thinking on world affairs. First, it embraced an enlarged internationalism: a strengthened commitment to measures designed to foster international order and reconciliation, and an acceptance of some restraints on Soviet state power. Second, Gorbachev emphasized the mutuality of security: it was no longer acceptable to seek security for one's own people by making other peoples feel less secure. Security, he asserted, "is indivisible. It is either equal security for all or none at all." Adversaries "must become partners and start looking jointly for a way to achieve universal security."[52] Third, Gorbachev downgraded military levers in the pursuit of foreign policy and called for a major demilitarization of international relations. In his speech to the United Nations in December 1988, he declared: "The use or threat of force can no longer be an instrument of foreign policy. This applies, above all, to nuclear arms. But that is not the only thing that matters. All of us, and primarily the stronger of us, must exercise

self-restraint and totally rule out any outward-oriented use of force."
It is clear, he continued, "that building up military power makes no
country omnipotent. What is more, one-sided reliance on military
power ultimately weakens other components of national security."[53]
He spoke in *Perestroika* of "the inflated role played by militarists in
politics."[54] Fourth, Gorbachev endorsed a political vision that
stressed the fact of global interdependence and the common perils
that, in his view, demanded common action. This vision was pressed
especially vigorously with regard to underdevelopment (or, more
bluntly, Third World poverty and misery) and ecological degrada-
tion. The consequences and implications of these evils were largely
indifferent to national boundaries and thus were potential destroyers
of citizens everywhere. As he put the matter metaphorically: "the
nations of the world resemble today a pack of mountaineers tied
together by a climbing rope. They can either climb on together to
the mountain peak or fall together into an abyss."[55]

Such ideas had rarely crossed the lips of political leaders, at least
in public. Why at that time? And why from Moscow? While there
were no doubt many reasons for Gorbachev's startling views, one
was the disastrous failure of so much of previous Soviet foreign and
military policy. Stalin's truculence and brutal despotism had, on the
whole, worsened his country's international position; and Khrushchev, though much more accommodating and much less tyran-
nical, had undermined some of his diplomatic efforts through in-
temperate muscle-flexing (with missiles and monster multi-megaton
н-bombs) and bellicose posturing. More recently, in the late Brezhnev years, Gorbachev and likeminded leaders must surely have been
sensitive to the dismal state of Moscow's relations with much of the
international community. (Ironically, these were the same years
when alarmist Americans were full of fear about a Moscow on the
march.) When the 1980s began, the Kremlin was on generally poor
terms with *all* the other major centres of power (that is, China, Japan,
Western Europe, the United States) and most of the Islamic world;
and it was faced with a major revolt in Poland, a crucial part of its
border with the West. These facts were hardly suggestive of a successful diplomacy. Indeed, they were striking testimonies (from any
undoctrinaire perspective) to the ineptness, lack of suppleness, un-
imaginativeness, and fundamental impoverishment of Soviet foreign
policy. So deficient and clumsy was Soviet policy in the early 1980s
that Washington under Reagan got something of a free ride in the
East-West rivalry – in a sense, the United States got an unearned
advantage, which was accentuated by the succession crises that hob-
bled the Kremlin during these years. Gorbachev inherited a sterile

set of foreign policies, and it seems that he was determined to make a radical break with this inglorious past.

Gorbachev gave particular attention to the role of nuclear weapons in world affairs. Essentially, he emphasized the perils of nuclear deterrence and called into question its political utility. He held that the imperative of avoiding nuclear war superseded the claims of class interest and revolutionary change. "With the emergence of weapons of mass, that is, universal destruction," he observed, "there appeared an objective limit for class confrontation in the international arena: the threat of universal destruction. For the first time ever there emerged a real, not speculative and remote, common human interest – to save humanity from disaster."[56] Gorbachev pushed this position towards an explicit scepticism concerning war as a meaningful political activity, whether fought with nuclear or non-nuclear weapons. Nuclear war, he thought, would clearly be senseless and irrational, but "military technology has developed to such an extent that even a non-nuclear war would now be comparable with a nuclear war in its destructive effect." Any sort of armed clash between the major powers was simply too risky to contemplate. Thus he concluded about post-Hiroshima world politics:

A new dialectic of strength and security follows from the impossibility of a military – that is, nuclear – solution to international differences. Security can no longer be assured by military means ... Attempts to achieve military superiority are preposterous ... From the security point of view the arms race has become an absurdity because its very logic leads to the destabilization of international relations and eventually to a nuclear conflict. Diverting huge resources from other priorities, the arms race is lowering the level of security, impairing it. It is in itself an enemy of peace. The only way to security is through political decisions and disarmament. In our age genuine and equal security can be guaranteed by constantly lowering the level of the strategic balance from which nuclear and other weapons of mass destruction should be completely eliminated.[57]

This new thinking by the Soviet leadership prompts several reflections. First, most of what Gorbachev had to say, however significant politically and surprising it was (and undoubtedly encouraging as well), was not new to those many Western intellectuals who at one time or another had commented on the politics of the nuclear age. In fact, whatever their immediate sources, almost all of Gorbachev's ideas can be found in previous North American and European writings – in the *Bulletin of the Atomic Scientists*, in the warnings of anti-nuclear observers, in passages from the works of some of the more thoughtful and prescient strategists. Some of this thinking has been referred to earlier in this book and more examples could be offered. With regard to the political relevance of war in the nuclear age, for example, as early as January 1953 a study entitled "Armaments and American Policy" presented to the United States secretary of state declared that "fundamentally, and in the long run, the problem which is posed by the release of atomic energy is a problem of the ability of the human race to govern itself without war."[58] If war made no sense, then what could be the long-term role of weapons of war? The arguments that critics of the heavily nuclear strategy of the United States had long put forward resurfaced more or less unchanged in the 1980s. In his book, *Strategy and Conscience*, published in 1964, Anatol Rapoport reasoned, as some others did as well, that "if destructiveness is directly related to the efficiency of weapons and to the willingness to use them, common sense would dictate that security lies in making weapons less efficient and in erecting inhibitions against their use, that is, in physical and ideological disarmament."[59] Scepticism about the long-term virtue of nuclear deterrence, which meant in practice the incessant "modernization" of the world's arsenals, had been voiced again and again in the 1950s and 1960s and found yet another voice in the 1980s, very unexpectedly, in Mikhail Gorbachev and his fellow reformers in the Soviet Union.

This critique of a nuclear-dependent strategy, whether from Gorbachev or elsewhere, was seen in many Western military circles as fundamentally subversive. Western strategy was wedded to nuclear weapons; United States doctrine and operational planning placed nuclear weapons at centre stage in thinking about security (by the 1980s the United States navy was as heavily nuclearized as the air force); and thus it was hardly surprising that the custodians and friends of these weapons were hostile to arguments that deprecated their merits. A telling instance of this state of mind was a remark made in late 1988 by General William Odom, director (1985–8) of the highly secretive National Security Agency and thus a leading member of President Reagan's national security élite. Speaking about the public sympathy for and attraction to Gorbachev's anti-nuclear pronouncements, Odom complained: "a denuclearization policy ... attacks the NATO doctrine of deterrence through nuclear weapons. Gorbachev's ideological innovation, insisting that nuclear weapons can have no political utility, means that U.S. deterrence doctrine is against the interests of mankind. Deterrence doctrine, of course, implies a political utility for nuclear weapons, a utility that Gorbachev's ideological proposition would take away."[60] General Odom regretted the welcome Gorbachev's ideas had received and hoped that the erosion of faith in deterrence could be effectively held in check.

American security policy had always been rather vulnerable to criticism because of its stress on the importance of nuclear weapons – though such criticism had commonly been brushed aside or disdained. After all, here was the United States, the world's leading liberal-industrial nation, which, on the one hand, presented itself as the champion of human rights and liberty and civilized values and, on the other hand, took *the* leading role in threatening nuclear devastation in order to preserve these rights and values and other interests deemed vital to the nation. Because of this official American position, the Soviet Union, from the start of the nuclear age, had often been able to stand on firmer and more coherent intellectual ground in formulating its positions on the nuclear threat. Consider the views of one early observer who touched on this delicate issue. Writing in 1951, Richard Stebbins remarked perceptively on the Soviet peace campaign that was then being conducted against the "immoral" atomic weapon. He, like most Americans, faulted this campaign (which, indeed, was heavily propagandistic) but conceded that "it undoubtedly encouraged the popular revulsion against atomic warfare and thus tended to build up the psychological obstacles to the use of the atomic bomb by the United States." He also noted the advantages the Soviet Union enjoyed in condemning nuclear weaponry: after "they managed to develop an atomic bomb," he thought, "they were unlikely to make it the centerpiece of their strategy, still less to announce the fact to a shuddering world ... they had everything to gain by playing upon the apprehensions which the American attitude had aroused in Western Europe and elsewhere."[61] In later years, of course, Moscow sometimes did choose to emulate the United States and flaunt its own nuclear missiles (rarely with any advantage to itself), though by the 1980s the Soviet leadership was again emphasizing the sort of anti-nuclear sentiment with which it had allied itself three decades earlier.

Gorbachev's innovations broke all sorts of new ground and drew attention to a lot of intellectual dust that had been collecting over the years, both at home and abroad. Those discomfited by these shake-ups were to be found in the West as well as in the East, for Gorbachev's initiatives went a long way to erode the threat consensus and Cold War assumptions that had propped up and legitimized the nuclear strategy of the United States and NATO. These Soviet initiatives also undermined public willingness in the West to finance ever more expensive and ever more exotic military hardware, especially in a nation which was heavily in debt. Western anti-communists were often both gratified and disconcerted by what was happening. On the one hand, Moscow's new words and actions seemed to acknowledge and confirm much of the long-standing Western critique of Soviet communism: a critique that focused on the arbitrary rule, bureaucratic constraints, economic stagnancy, lack of human rights, and suffocating conformity in the USSR. On the other hand, while Gorbachev was breaking with Soviet traditions of smugness and self-serving ideological pieties, his efforts in the late 1980s also showed up the staleness of much of what passed for strategic thinking in the West and the inertia that gripped so many Western institutional and bureaucratic interests. While change for the better in the Soviet Union was probably going to mean major political and intellectual surgery, which the West certainly did not see itself as having to undergo, it was nonetheless quite clear that a lot of the orthodox wisdom in Washington and the allied capitals concerning national and international security look tired, out of date, and unimaginative – perhaps even irrelevant to the changing needs of the times. For many Western military interests, the Cold War embodied a professionally congenial sense of permanent crisis and a clear recognition of the permanent enemy. A much diminished sense of crisis and a much less hostile enemy were not necessarily welcome, for they tended to pull the rug out from under the basic premises of the Pentagon, the NATO establishment, and their many civilian associates in the media and among "defence intellectuals." These were years in which the centrality and plausibility of resolutely military modes of thought about the planet were losing credibility, and certain vested interests were bound not to profit from these changes.

The defensiveness of these entrenched military interests certainly contributed to the immobility of American security policy in the late 1980s. On the one hand, public opinion (especially in Europe) had come to the conclusion that the Soviet Union posed little political threat, that the prospect of a Soviet military attack against the West was completely implausible (it never really had been all that credible), and that Moscow was redeploying its armed forces in a manner that virtually precluded a surprise assault by the Warsaw pact. And yet Washington responded very, very slowly to these momentous developments. During George Bush's first months as president in 1989, there were hardly any perceptible changes in United States strategic doctrine, nuclear targeting, or weapons procurement. Richard Cheney, the new secretary of defense, continued to demand, as had Caspar Weinberger earlier in the decade, that Congress fully fund just about every nuclear weapons programme that had been launched in previous years; otherwise, he asserted, America's security would be gravely imperilled. This stance meant big appropriations for two land-based missiles, the MX in some mobile mode and the non-MIRVed (but expensive) Midgetman, as well as the spectacularly expensive B-2 bomber. Meanwhile, the Strategic Defense Initiative was still being presented as a vital key to the nation's future, even as its faithful supporters dwindled. Some people were arguing in 1989 that, as a result of the remarkable improvements in East-West relations, there really was a good possibility that United States military requirements could be dramatically reduced; but this was not a possibility that sat well with those powerful interests and local constituencies that were used to receiving the Pentagon's bounty. A modest nuclear establishment was *not* what the American state had inherited from the preceding forty years. Downsizing this nuclear behemoth, it was clear, was likely to be neither politically easy nor universally applauded.

Another point of note is that Soviet thinking in the 1980s, in contrast to mainstream Western thinking, repeatedly called into question the supposed stability of deterrence and emphasized the possibility of nuclear catastrophe through inadvertence or miscalculation. The Soviet Union probably tended to be more sensitive than most Westerners to the danger of war erupting unintentionally: that is, the risk that war might come about as a result of a conflict getting out of control or of an unauthorized or rash military action that might trigger a conflagration that all parties actually wanted to avoid. Gorbachev and his associates strongly emphasized these hazards – as did some American experts, though more insistently as a rule if they were out of government (and thus less influential) than in it. Nuclear weapons placed an extraordinary concentration of destructive force in ordinary human hands; and the new Soviet thinking tended to draw particular attention to what might happen if fallible human beings, as a result of negligence or folly, misjudgment or panic, acted in a way that released this force upon the world. The possibility of glitches, bungling, or imprudence seemed on the whole to weigh more heavily on the Soviet than the American official mind (the latter always made much of the lesson of Munich and thus the necessity always to stand tall and never to appease). Whatever the shallow optimism of official Soviet ideology, the deeper culture of Russia was more pessimistic about the human condition than the culture of the United States. Past experience made the Soviet Union much less sanguine about the avoidance of accidents than did that of the United States, and Soviet history, in contrast to the buoyant history of the United States, was replete with terrible man-made disasters. These circumstances may account in part for Moscow's thinking on the possible causes of nuclear war.

Finally, the new thinking of the late 1980s, in Moscow and increasingly in the West as well, stressed the indivisibility of life in the nuclear age. In his "Open Letter to the United Nations" in June 1950, the great Danish physicist and humanist, Niels Bohr, had spoken of how "the progress of science and technology has tied the fate of all nations inseparably together."[62] Some forty years later the truth of this statement was so obvious as to be beyond dispute. As societies struggled to cope with a whole range of social and environmental problems (deforestation, desertification, waste disposal, acid rain, species extinction, ozone depletion), the interconnectedness of human life on a small planet seemed more and more self-evident and the right to unilateral national self-assertion less and less persuasive (at least objectively, for fervent nationalisms still had much subjective appeal).

A larger, more global view was clearly essential. A former American astronaut, writing in 1987, was one of those who remarked on the need for a more unified perspective, to accord with the unity of nature. He spoke from personal experience of a "revelation that comes from circling this planet": "As you pass from sunlight into darkness and back again every hour and a half, you become startlingly aware how artificial are the thousands of boundaries we've created to separate and define. And for the first time in your life you feel in your gut the precious unity of the earth and all the living things it supports. The dissonance between this unity you see and the separateness of human groupings that you know exists is starkly apparent."[63] As far-sighted observers had been saying repeatedly since 1945 and in a few cases even earlier, this dissonance could not persist indefinitely; it would have to be confronted creatively, and better sooner than later, given the potentially disastrous costs of delay (increasingly a real possibility). In the late 1980s, there were at least some signs that these warnings were starting to be heard and digested and occasionally even translated into constructive political action.

Epilogue

On 21 February 1944, Marie Vassiltchikov, a young woman of White Russian descent living in Berlin, a city whose inhabitants had been under siege for several months from waves of allied bombers, attended a movie and recorded her feelings in her diary. "This evening we saw *Ochsenkrieg* [War of Oxen], a film about war in the Middle Ages. It was particularly restful to see people whacking away at one another with wooden clubs. After five or six hours' fighting the battlefield was strewn with seven bodies!"[1] While systematic violence was nothing new, the tools of violence certainly were. What was remarkable to the endangered Miss Vassiltchikov and would be widely regarded by the end of that war as even more remarkable was the lethality of the modern machinery of death. Science had abolished the limits on killing, thereby ensuring that destruction on virtually any scale would henceforth be attainable. The scientifically managed Nazi extermination camps as well as saturation air bombardment gave their victims a stark sense of the potency of modern science. After Hiroshima the prospect of the destruction of the earth had to be confronted by everyone. War had run a devastating course through the first half of the twentieth century; in the second half of the century the potential tragic consequences of any future widespread war had reached unspeakable, almost unimaginable proportions.

In this modern world, the battlefield was potentially everywhere. Much of the conventional understanding of war had been rendered obsolete, for there were in fact no defences, no means of protection, no barriers to blunt attacks, no shields to take shelter behind, no boundaries between the field of battle and the field of normal life. Moreover, this momentous development had occurred very abruptly. There had been no time to adjust to it, no time to ponder its implications, and no time to acclimatize (especially intellectually and emotionally) to the new conditions of existence. These conditions were so startling and so shattering of established conventions that the experience of the past was often of little use as a guide to present or future conduct. The rules of life had been thrown into confusion. As one writer said of the world's first atomic explosion, the Trinity test in the Alamogordo desert of New Mexico on 16 July 1945: "In the instant of that blast, humans became fantastically powerful and fantastically vulnerable."[2] In these extraordinary conditions, a policy of business as usual was bound to be less than convincing.

It has been this ambiguity of power that people have reflected upon again and again since 1945. Science has yielded power – the power to create and master and ameliorate, and also the power to destroy indiscriminately. Nature is more at man's mercy than ever before and its brute forces are in certain respects more under human control; but at the same time, in tampering with nature, in exercising a partial lordship over it, mankind risks a backlash from nature and is now in constant danger of having to pay a crippling price for incautious and arrogant or even merely miscalculated interventions. Modern power means both control over nature and the ever present peril that this power might escape control and consume its possessors. "The essential problem of the nuclear age," as one author put it, "derives from our seizure of the ultimate powers of nature." This problem is now a permanent fixture of the human condition. What we have learned cannot be expunged from our minds: "This power is now part of our very being; it cannot be lost."[3]

It is worth recalling an observation made in 1961 by Thomas Schelling and Morton Halperin, the authors of one of the first serious treatises on nuclear weaponry and arms control. "Man's capability for self-destruction," they remarked, "cannot be eradicatd – he knows too much! Keeping that capability under control – providing incentives to minimize recourse to violence – is the eternal challenge."[4] This is the heart of the nuclear predicament. The capacity for self-destruction is probably inescapable; what is known cannot be made unknown. The permanent problem this knowledge has created is the problem of ensuring that this capacity for self-destruction is never actually realized. But how can a capacity for a certain action be permanently suppressed? How can a lid be kept indefinitely on the capacity for catastrophic violence?

These are questions that should be central to current political debates. And in confronting them and in striving (at the least) to avoid the worst and keep disaster at bay, we will certainly be in need of enlarged political imaginations. This intellectual task will also require a critical assessment of what we have inherited and at least a partial break with the nuclearized traditions of the past. In the future, nuclear threats should have a much lower profile: the nuclear threat posture, rather than being accentuated, ought to be reduced and eventually minimized. The importance of what is referred to as security through mutual deterrence and mutual threats can be and, in the long term, must be diminished and substantially replaced by relations of mutual assurance. This would mean not only discouraging recourse to violence in general but also strengthening international law as a mediating force between nation-states, such that over time law would become the pre-eminent mode of mediation in international relations. Talk about peace is cheap and often fraudulent; the talk that is serious and constructive is that which concerns the designing of procedures to manage and contain the inevitable conflicts among nations. Given the explosiveness and ferocity of war in the nuclear age, the only alternative to a future of prolonged anarchy or suicidal combat is law. But law cannot be created overnight. It has to emerge out of the experiences and self-awareness of peoples who share a certain common grounding and a common sense of peril. Translating these elements of commonality into sound policies remains the critical imperative.

Stanley Hoffmann, one of the most thoughtful academic commentators on international affairs, proposed in 1985 that what was needed, "both among intellectuals and in statecraft, is a *quest for a new realism*, one that acknowledges the stark realities of a divided world, yet tries – through cooperation and collective action in a variety of fields – to change the game sufficiently to prevent revolutionary hurricanes and nuclear explosions from destroying it, and us, altogether. A realism of 'the struggle for power' is not enough. A realism of struggle *and* world order has yet to emerge."[5] It is this pursuit of a reasonable and just world order that is now imperative. The nuclear threat is only one of many manifestations of our new state of global interdependence, which itself is largely a product of science, both military and non-military. National sovereignty has been rendered partly obsolete; human security is largely unrelated to crude military force; and there are no strictly military solutions to the problems created by our own destructive power. Survival will depend on greater political wisdom; less reliance on threats and more on reconciliation; and an enhanced recognition that internationalism, mutuality, and political self-restraint offer the only promising paths to an endurable future. Rivalries, of course, will persist. But in a world that is both wired to explode and drifting toward any number of environmental disasters, competitiveness must be complemented by collaboration and muted by a deepened and fortified sense of common interests. A planet dominated by the rules of power politics has only a bleak future. Unless these rules can be overhauled, the fittest to survive may not even be human, much less the best of human civilization.

Notes

ABBREVIATIONS

FRUS *Foreign Relations of the United States* (Washington DC: United States Government Printing Office)
BAS *Bulletin of the Atomic Scientists*

CHAPTER ONE

1 Brien E. McMahon, "Atomic Weapons and Defense," *BAS* 7 (October 1951): 298.
2 Sir John Slessor, *The Central Blue: Recollections and Reflections* (London: Cassell 1956), 637.
3 Sir John Slessor, *Strategy for the West* (London: Cassell 1954), 69 and 16.
4 *Public Papers of the Presidents of the United States: Harry S. Truman: April 12 to December 31, 1945* (Washington DC: United States Government Printing Office 1961), 200.
5 *Survival in the Air Age: A Report by the President's Air Policy Commission* (Washington DC: United States Government Printing Office, 1 January 1948), 8. A similar position was enunciated later that year in a National Security Council report, "United States Policy on Atomic Warfare," *FRUS, 1948*, vol. I, part 2 (1976), 626–7.
6 Ibid., 750.
7 *FRUS, 1946*, vol. I (1972), 1203. Groves's influence is documented in many passages of Gregg Herken, *The Winning Weapon: The Atomic Bomb in the Cold War 1945–1950* (New York: Knopf 1980).
8 Memorandum of John D. Hickerson, assistant secretary of state for United Nations affairs, 11 January 1950, in *FRUS, 1950*, vol. I, part 2

(1977), 11. Such complacency was perhaps more the norm than the exception. In a lecture given in May 1948, some fifteen months before the first Soviet atomic test, Bernard Brodie, normally one of the most astute of the early strategic thinkers, emphasized the possibility of long-term American atomic superiority: "It is too generally forgotten that our position vis-à-vis the Soviet Union in atomic warfare will be much better on the day the Russians produce their first bomb than it is at present, for the simple reason that we will then have many more bombs, perhaps several times as many, as we do now ... our *superiority* will increase considerably before it begins to wane; it may continue to increase even after the Soviet Union is producing bombs; and it may be a long time in waning thereafter. If the raw materials available in the world for the production of atomic bombs are as limited as some seem to think, this situation [of superiority] may be a permanent one, that is, it may not in our time [be significantly lost]." He thought that "the enormous technological lead which the United States has over the Soviet Union and which shows no immediate signs of diminishing is bound to mean a great potential advantage for the United States in the design of the instruments for using the atomic bomb." "New Techniques of War and National Policies," in William F. Ogburn, ed., *Technology and International Relations* (Chicago: University of Chicago Press 1949), 155 and 164.

9 Thomas K. Finletter, *Power and Policy: U.S. Foreign Policy and Military Power in the Hydrogen Age* (New York: Harcourt, Brace 1954), 298 and 299.

10 James H. Douglas, "Air Power and Foreign Policy," in Eugene M. Emme, ed., *The Impact of Air Power: National Security and World Politics* (Princeton NJ: Van Nostrand 1959), 802.

11 Thomas E. Murray, "Don't Leave Atomic Energy to the Experts," BAS 10 (February 1954): 49.

12 Richard P. Stebbins, *The United States in World Affairs, 1953* (New York: Harper for the Council on Foreign Relations 1955), 358.

13 Robert Strausz-Hupé, "Foreword," *Annals of the American Academy of Political and Social Science* 299 (May 1955): vii.

14 Stefan Possony, *Strategic Air Power: The Pattern of Dynamic Security* (Washington DC: Infantry Journal Press 1949), 308.

15 Dale O. Smith, *U.S. Military Doctrine: A Study and Appraisal* (New York: Duell, Sloan and Pearce 1955), 167 and 142. See also the important testimony in Richard H. Kohn and Joseph P. Harahan, eds., "U.S. Strategic Air Power, 1948–1962: Excerpts from an Interview with Generals Curtis E. LeMay, Leon W. Johnson, David A. Burchinal, and Jack J. Catton," *International Security* 12, no. 4 (spring 1988), 78–95.

16 Eugene M. Emme, in *Impact of Air Power*, 605–6.

17 Bonner Fellers, *Wings for Peace: A Primer for a New Defense* (Chicago: Regnery 1953), 246 and 248. For an extreme espousal of the general position documented in this chapter largely from official or quasi-official sources, see Alexander P. de Seversky, *Air Power: Key to Survival* (New York: Simon and Schuster 1950). Seversky argued that "the manifest destiny of the United States is in the skies. We must attain a superiority in the air that can be as great a force for world peace as Britain's superiority on the seas in its day." (p 349) In his view, "a correct strategy, aiming at global command of the entire air space, is now possible and within our capacity." (p 352) "We have what it takes," he thought, "to forge the weapons of victory and of lasting peace. The decision rests with the American people. Nothing less than human freedom, for ourselves and all mankind, is at stake." (p 356) General Thomas D. White, chief of staff of the USAF, presented a similar argument in favour of "the pre-eminence of air power" in a speech given in November 1957, which is reprinted in Emme, ed., *Impact of Air Power*, 496–501.

18 Paul Boyer, *By the Bomb's Early Light: American Thought and Culture at the Dawn of the Atomic Age* (New York: Pantheon 1985), 327.

19 Ibid., 349. Chapters 26 and 27 of Boyer's book are particularly informative on this changed sensibility. See also H. Bruce Franklin, *War Stars: The Superweapon and the American Imagination* (New York: Oxford University Press 1988), especially 116–17. Oppenheimer's remarks are in his essay, "Atomic Weapons," *Proceedings of the American Philosophical Society* 90, no. 1 (January 1946): 7.

20 *New York Times*, 1 September 1950, 4.

21 Ibid., 6 April 1954, 28.

22 Steven L. Rearden, *History of the Office of the Secretary of Defense*. I: *The Formative Years 1947–1950* (Washington DC: Office of the Secretary of Defense 1984), 438; and David Alan Rosenberg, "The Origins of Overkill: Nuclear Weapons and American Strategy," in Norman A. Graebner, ed., *The National Security: Its Theory and Practice 1945–1960* (New York: Oxford University Press 1986), 141–2.

23 *FRUS, 1952–1954*, vol. v, part 1 (1983), 512, and *Department of State Bulletin* 33 (3 January 1955): 14 (remarks made at a news conference on 21 December 1954); cf. Robert H. Ferrell, ed., *The Diary of James C. Hagerty: Eisenhower in Mid-Course, 1954–1955* (Bloomington IN: Indiana University Press 1983), 211.

24 John Colville, *The Fringes of Power: Downing Street Diaries 1939–1955* (London: Hodder and Stoughton 1985), 685–6; Richard K. Betts, *Nuclear Blackmail and Nuclear Balance* (Washington DC: Brookings Institu-

tion 1987), 40–1 and 46–7; and John Lewis Gaddis, *The Long Peace: Inquiries into the History of the Cold War* (New York: Oxford University Press 1987), 136–7 and 140–1.

25 Col. George C. Reinhardt, *American Strategy in the Atomic Age* (Norman OK: University of Oklahoma Press 1955), 58.

26 Smith, *U.S. Military Doctrine*, 185.

27 James H. Doolittle, "Science and Airpower," in John F. Loosbrock and Richard M. Skinner, eds., *The Wild Blue: The Story of American Airpower* (New York: Putnam's 1961), 415; reprinted from *Air Force Magazine* (June 1953).

28 Reinhardt, *American Strategy*, 58.

29 *FRUS, 1951*, vol. I (1979), 158–9.

30 Roger M. Anders, ed., *Forging the Atomic Shield: Excerpts from the Office Diary of Gordon E. Dean* (Chapel Hill NC: University of North Carolina Press 1987), appendix, 281–2.

31 Smith, *U.S. Military Doctrine*, 178–9; and T.F. Walkowitz, "Strategic Concepts for the Nuclear Age," *Annals of the American Academy of Political and Social Science* 299 (May 1955): 124. For an authoritative and admirably informative account of the development of American policies on tactical nuclear weapons during these years, see Matthew Evangelista, *Innovation and the Arms Race: How the United States and the Soviet Union Develop New Military Technologies* (Ithaca NY: Cornell University Press 1988), chap. 4. Also valuable is Jane E. Stromseth, *The Origins of Flexible Response: NATO's Debate over Strategy in the 1960s* (New York: St Martin's 1988), chap. 2.

32 Edward C. Keefer, "President Dwight D. Eisenhower and the End of the Korean War," *Diplomatic History* 10, no. 3 (summer 1986): 272–3; and *FRUS, 1952–1954*, vol. XV, part 1 (1984), 770 and 827.

33 Robert C. Richardson III, "Atomic Bombs and War Damage," *Orbis* 4, no. 1 (spring 1960): 40–2; see also 51–3. One of the most influential and widely read arguments in favour of tactical nuclear warfare, which also assumed effective damage limitation, was presented by Henry A. Kissinger in his *Nuclear Weapons and Foreign Policy* (New York: Harper for the Council on Foreign Relations 1957); see especially chap. 6.

34 Richard G. Hewlett and Jack M. Holl, *Atoms for Peace and War, 1953–1961: Eisenhower and the Atomic Energy Commission* (Berkeley and Los Angeles: University of California Press 1989), 18–19.

35 Anders, ed., *Forging the Atomic Shield*, 271; and Glenn T. Seaborg, with Benjamin S. Loeb, *Stemming the Tide: Arms Control in the Johnson Years* (Lexington MA: Lexington Books 1987), 21 (see also 25–32).

36 Thomas B. Cochran, William M. Arkin, and Milton M. Hoenig, *Nu-*

clear Weapons Databook. 1: *U.S. Nuclear Forces and Capabilities* (Cambridge MA: Ballinger 1984), 15.

37 Richard P. Stebbins, *The United States in World Affairs, 1958* (New York: Harper for the Council on Foreign Relations 1959), 102.

38 For evidence on early Soviet concerns about the atomic bomb, see *FRUS, 1945,* vol. v (1967), 922–4; W. Averell Harriman and Elie Abel, *Special Envoy to Churchill and Stalin 1941–1946* (London: Hutchinson 1976), 519; *Documents on British Policy Overseas,* Series I, Volume II: *Conferences and Conversations 1945* (London: Her Majesty's Stationery Office 1985), 534, 569–70, and 650–2; and David Holloway, "Entering the Nuclear Arms Race: The Soviet Decision to Build the Atomic Bomb, 1939–45," *Social Studies of Science* 11, no. 2 (May 1981): 184–5.

39 Strobe Talbott, trans. and ed., *Khrushchev Remembers: The Last Testament* (Boston: Little, Brown 1974), 58.

40 On preventive war, see Robert W. Malcolmson, *Nuclear Fallacies: How We Have Been Misguided since Hiroshima* (Kingston and Montreal: McGill-Queen's University Press 1985), 46–9 and 136; John Morton Blum, ed., *The Price of Vision: The Diary of Henry A. Wallace, 1942–1946* (Boston: Houghton Mifflin 1973), 534–5; Richard P. Stebbins, *The United States in World Affairs, 1949* (New York: Harper for the Council on Foreign Relations 1950), 11n; Sir John Slessor, "The Chances of War" (1948), in *The Great Deterrent* (London: Cassell 1957), 100–1; B.H. Liddell Hart, *Defence of the West* (London: Cassell 1950), 149; and Alastair Buchan, *War in Modern Society* (London: C.A. Watts 1966), 43.

41 Slessor, "Chances of War," 89.

42 *FRUS, 1951,* vol. I (1979), 848.

43 Smith, *U.S. Military Doctrine,* 166.

44 Melvin R. Laird, *A House Divided: America's Strategy Gap* (Chicago IL: Regnery 1962), 78–9.

45 Thomas H. Etzold and John Lewis Gaddis, eds., *Containment: Documents on American Policy and Strategy, 1945–1950* (New York: Columbia University Press 1978), 370.

46 Emme, ed., *Impact of Air Power,* 500.

47 Gregg Herken, *Counsels of War* (New York: Knopf 1985), 96 (see, in general, the discussion at 96–8); see also Ted Greenwood, *Making the MIRV: A Study of Defense Decision Making* (Cambridge MA: Ballinger 1975), 58, and Betts, *Nuclear Blackmail,* 161–3.

48 David Alan Rosenberg, "Reality and Responsibility: Power and Process in the Making of United States Nuclear Strategy, 1945–68," *Journal of Strategic Studies* 9, no. 1 (March 1986): 40.

49 Rosenberg, "Origins of Overkill," in Graebner, ed., *National Security,* 174. For similar evidence from 1961, see Scott D. Sagan,

"Siop–62: The Nuclear War Plan Briefing to President Kennedy," *International Security* 12, no. 1 (summer 1987); 22–51.

50 Nathan F. Twining, *Neither Liberty nor Safety: A Hard Look at U.S. Military Policy and Strategy* (New York: Holt, Rinehart and Winston 1966), 100. "Unfortunately," he added, and here he was expressing many officers' disenchantment with the policies of the then secretary of defense, Robert McNamara, "the conviction that no one can win a nuclear war does much to pull the force, drive, and sense of urgency from American research and development programs and it also adversely affects u.s. force structure in being. There is no question that a nuclear war can be 'won', as wars of the past have been won – by the side which is best prepared to fight it." (p 112)

51 Brent Scowcroft, "Deterrence and Strategic Superiority," *Orbis* 13, no. 2 (summer 1969), 439 (Scowcroft, then a usaf colonel, later became a general and national security adviser to Presidents Ford and Bush); Fred Charles Iklé, "Can Nuclear Deterrence Last Out the Century?" *Foreign Affairs* 51, no. 2 (January 1973): 277; and Roger Speed, *Strategic Deterrence in the 1980s* (Stanford ca: Hoover Institution Press 1979), 8. It is noteworthy that Bernard Brodie, who was one of the first strategists to question the war-fighting and war-winning significance of nuclear weapons, and who in 1945–6 foresaw the political stalemate that these weapons were likely to bring about, was by the later 1950s pointing to the merits of a large nuclear arsenal; for, he said, "our retaliatory force must also be capable of striking first, and if it does so its attack had better be, as nearly as possible, overwhelming to the enemy's retaliatory force." (*Strategy in the Missile Age* [Princeton nj: Princeton University Press 1959], 277.)

52 Hans J. Morgenthau, *American Foreign Policy: A Critical Examination* (London: Methuen 1952), 7.

53 *Public Papers of Truman 1945*, 213.

54 Ibid., 437.

55 The authors of a strategic studies text published by the Foreign Policy Research Institute even presumed that Moscow endorsed Washington's self-assessments. "We can be sure," they wrote, "that Soviet strategists understand full well that the u.s. overseas base structure is a defensive-retaliatory instrument and not an offensive-pre-emptive one. They can properly estimate our strategic intentions. They can do so confidently because we are an open society." (Robert Strausz-Hupé, William R. Kintner, and Stefan T. Possony, *A Forward Strategy for America* [New York: Harper 1961], 312.) As we have seen, pre-emption was, in fact, a major component of American strategy.

56 Anders, ed., *Forging the Atomic Shield*, 279–80.

57 Tami R. Davis and Sean M. Lynn-Jones, "'Citty Upon a Hill'," *Foreign Policy*, no. 66 (spring 1987): 20–38.
58 Smith, *U.S. Military Doctrine*, 189. He added: "If moral forces reject the use of atomic weapons, an open invitation is tendered to the immoral forces to take over."
59 Robert E. Osgood, *Ideals and Self-Interest in America's Foreign Relations* (Chicago: University of Chicago Press 1953), 444.
60 Reinhold Niebuhr, *Christian Realism and Political Problems* (New York: Scribner's 1953), 30. The British military writer, B.H. Liddell Hart, offered a similar warning: "Avoid self-righteousness like the devil – nothing is so self-blinding." (*Deterrent or Defence* [London: Stevens 1960], 248.)
61 Among the most useful works on strategic bombing are the following: Martin Middlebrook, *The Nuremberg Raid, 30–31 March 1944* (London: Allen Lane 1973) and *The Battle of Hamburg: Allied Bomber Forces against a German City in 1943* (London: Allen Lane 1980); Max Hastings, *Bomber Command* (New York: Dial Press/James Wade 1979); Ronald Schaffer, *Wings of Judgment: American Bombing in World War II* (New York: Oxford University Press 1985); Michael S. Sherry, "Was 1945 a Break in History?" *BAS* 43 (July/August 1987): 12–15, and *The Rise of American Air Power: The Creation of Armageddon* (New Haven CT: Yale University Press 1987).
62 University of California at Los Angeles, Research Library, Bernard Brodie Papers, box 20, file 13 (Munich Conference, February 1968), typescript paper, "Nuclear Strategy in Its Political Context," 1.
63 Herbert F. York, *Making Weapons, Talking Peace: A Physicist's Odyssey from Hiroshima to Geneva* (New York: Basic Books 1987), 194.

CHAPTER TWO

1 John Morton Blum, ed., *The Price of Vision: The Diary of Henry A. Wallace, 1942–1946* (Boston: Houghton Mifflin 1973), 471.
2 *FRUS, 1952–1954*, vol. II, part 2 (1984), 1071.
3 Ibid., 1080.
4 McGeorge Bundy, *Danger and Survival: Choices about the Bomb in the First Fifty Years* (New York: Random House 1988), 301 and 299.
5 Quoted in H.W. Brands, Jr, *Cold Warriors: Eisenhower's Generation and American Foreign Policy* (New York: Columbia University Press 1988), 142–3.
6 National Archives of Canada, W.L.M. King Papers, MG 26, J1, 389, "Canadian Memorandum on Atomic Warfare," 349941.
7 *FRUS, 1952–1954*, vol. II, part 2 (1984), 1173–4.

8 Ibid., vol. II, part 1 (1984), 773.

9 Gordon Dean, "Tasks for the Statesmen," *BAS* 10 (January 1954): 11.

10 Hans Speier, *German Rearmament and Atomic War: The Views of German Military and Political Leaders* (Evanston IL: Row, Peterson 1957), 116–17.

11 For an excellent discussion of preventive war, see Marc Trachtenberg, "A 'Wasting Asset': American Strategy and the Shifting Nuclear Balance, 1949–1954," *International Security* 13, no. 3 (winter 1988/89): 5–49. See also his "Strategic Thought in America, 1952–1966," *Political Science Quarterly* 104, no. 2 (summer 1989): 314–15; and Tami Davis Biddle, "Handling the Soviet Threat: 'Project Control' and the Debate on American Strategy in the Early Cold War Years," *Journal of Strategic Studies* 12, no. 3 (September 1989): 274–8.

12 Dean, "Tasks for the Statesmen," 11.

13 Allan M. Winkler, "A 40-Year History of Civil Defense," *BAS* 40 (June/ July 1984): 16–22; Paul Boyer, *By the Bomb's Early Light: American Thought and Culture at the Dawn of the Atomic Age* (New York: Pantheon 1985), chap. 26; and JoAnne Brown, "Civil Defense in American Public Education, 1948–1963," *Journal of American History* 75, no. 1 (June 1988): 68–90. *No Place to Hide* (1948) was written by David Bradley.

14 A good guide to this debate and summary of the arguments is Martha J. Smith, "The Debate over Strategic Defenses, 1967–1987: A Study of American Ideology and Perspectives on National Security" (MA thesis, Queen's University, 1988), especially chap. 1.

15 Eugene Rabinowitch, "The Narrowing Way," *BAS* 9 (October 1953): 294.

16 James R. Killian, Jr, *Sputnik, Scientists, and Eisenhower: A Memoir of the First Special Assistant to the President for Science and Technology* (Cambridge MA: MIT Press 1977), 2–3.

17 United Kingdom, Public Record Office, FO 371, no. 132324, report by Sir Harold Caccia of 11 January 1958. The previous British ambassador to the United States, Sir Roger Makins, had thought, in July 1955, that "there is no fear of the Russians as such; indeed, the tendency here, in my view, is to under-rate rather than over-rate their strength." (FO 371, no. 114364, AU. 1022/16)

18 Henry A. Kissinger, *The Necessity for Choice: Prospects of American Foreign Policy* (New York: Harper and Row 1961), 15–16, 26, 36, and 102. For a useful guide to these debates, see Edgar M. Bottome, *The Missile Gap: A Study of the Formulation of Military and Political Policy* (Rutherford NJ: Fairleigh Dickinson University Press 1971).

19 Albert Wohlstetter, "The Delicate Balance of Terror," *Foreign Affairs* 37, no. 2 (January 1959): 211–34.

20 Raymond L. Garthoff, *Intelligence Assessment and Policy Making: A Deci-*

sion Point in the Kennedy Administration (Washington DC: Brookings Institution 1984), 27, and "Cuban Missile Crisis: The Soviet Story," *Foreign Policy*, no. 72 (fall 1988): 66.

21 Morton H. Halperin, *Limited War in the Nuclear Age* (New York: John Wiley 1963), 14.

22 Speier, *German Rearmament*, 116.

23 William R. Kintner, *Peace and the Strategy Conflict* (New York: Praeger 1967), 3.

24 Nathan F. Twining, *Neither Liberty nor Safety: A Hard Look at U.S. Military Policy and Strategy* (New York: Holt, Rinehart and Winston 1966), 164. Among the various other hawkish critiques of deterrence during the 1960s were the following: Thomas S. Power, *Design for Survival* (New York: Coward-McCann 1965); Curtis E. LeMay, with Dale O. Smith, *America Is in Danger* (New York: Funk and Wagnalls 1968); Melvin R. Laird, *A House Divided: America's Strategy Gap* (Chicago: Regnery 1962); Stefan T. Possony, "Toward a Strategy of Supremacy," in David M. Abshire and Richard V. Allen, eds., *National Security: Political, Military and Economic Strategies in the Decade Ahead* (New York: Praeger 1963), 535–65; and two books by Phyllis Schlafly and Chester Ward, *Strike from Space: How the Russians May Destroy Us* (New York: Devin-Adair 1966), and *The Gravediggers* (Alton IL: Pere Marquette Press 1964).

25 Barry M. Goldwater, *Why Not Victory? A Fresh Look at American Foreign Policy* (New York: McGraw-Hill 1962), 119–20.

26 Admiral Sir Gerald Dickens, *Bombing and Strategy: The Fallacy of Total War* (London, n.d. [c. 1946]), 66–7.

27 Fleet Admiral William D. Leahy, *I Was There: The Personal Story of the Chief of Staff to Presidents Roosevelt and Truman* (London: Gollancz 1950), 514–15.

28 John C. Campbell, *The United States in World Affairs, 1947–1948* (New York: Harper for the Council on Foreign Relations 1948), 15.

29 John H. Herz, *International Politics in the Atomic Age* (New York: Columbia University Press 1959), 22 (emphasis added).

30 Henry Kissinger, *White House Years* (Boston: Little, Brown 1979), 66.

31 John Foster Dulles, "A Policy of Boldness," *Life*, 19 May 1952, 152.

32 George F. Kennan, *Russia, the Atom, and the West* (London: Oxford University Press 1958), 56.

33 George F. Kennan, "American Diplomacy and the Military," in his *American Diplomacy*, expanded ed. (Chicago: University of Chicago Press 1984), 171–2.

34 William Attwood, *The Twilight Struggle: Tales of the Cold War* (New York: Harper and Row 1987), 157.

35 "American Policy in the New Phase of the Cold War," a report issued

by the Committee on International Policy of the National Planning Association, 10 December 1954, and forwarded by the British embassy in Washington to the Foreign Office in London (Public Record Office, FO 371, no. 114364, AU. 1022/1, 13).

36 Eugene Rabinowitch, "Ten Years That Changed the World," BAS 12 (January 1956), 4.

37 Bernard Brodie, Strategy in the Missile Age (Princeton NJ: Princeton University Press 1959), 397, 398.

38 John J. McCloy, "Foreword" to Henry L. Roberts, Russia and America: Dangers and Prospects (New York: Harper for the Council on Foreign Relations 1956), xxv.

39 G.F. Hudson, The Hard and Bitter Peace: World Politics since 1945 (London: Pall Mall Press 1966), 280.

40 Rabinowitch, "Ten Years That Changed the World," 5.

41 Coral Bell, Survey of International Affairs 1954 (London: Oxford University Press for the Royal Institute of International Affairs 1957), 123.

CHAPTER THREE

1 Adam B. Ulam, The Rivals: America and Russia since World War II (New York: Viking Press 1971), 382.

2 Both books were edited by Kenneth A. Oye, Donald Rothchild, and Robert J. Lieber. Eagle Entangled was published in 1979 by Longman (New York), Eagle Defiant in 1983 by Little, Brown (Boston).

3 Kenneth W. Thompson, "The Coming of the Third World War: A Review Essay," Political Science Quarterly 94, no. 4 (winter 1979–80): 669–70.

4 "Reagan Interview," in Robert Scheer, With Enough Shovels: Reagan, Bush and Nuclear War (New York: Random House 1982), 245.

5 Ibid., 251.

6 University of California at Los Angeles, Research Library, Bernard Brodie Papers, box 33, file 6, Japan Lectures, 1978 (never delivered), Lecture 6, 10 (draft typescript).

7 Robert G. Kaiser, "U.S.-Soviet Relations: Goodbye to Détente," Foreign Affairs 59, no. 3 (America and the World 1980): 505.

8 As of late 1989, some of the major sources on nuclear weapons policies and arms control during the Reagan years, in addition to the periodical literature and abundance of analytical essays, were John Newhouse, War and Peace in the Nuclear Age (New York: Knopf 1989), chaps. 12 and 13; two books by Strobe Talbott, Deadly Gambits: The Reagan Administration and the Stalemate in Nuclear Arms Control (New York: Knopf 1984) and The Master of the Game: Paul Nitze and the Nu-

clear Peace (New York: Knopf 1988); Hedrick Smith, *The Power Game: How Washington Works* (New York: Random House 1988), chaps. 15 and 16; Barry R. Posen and Stephen W. Van Evera, "Reagan Administration Defense Policy: Departure from Containment," in Kenneth A. Oye, Robert J. Lieber, and Donald Rothchild, eds., *Eagle Resurgent? The Reagan Era in American Foreign Policy* (Boston: Little, Brown 1987), 75–114; and Michael Krepon, *Arms Control in the Reagan Administration* (Lanham MD: University Press of America 1989).

9 Robert S. Flum, Sr, "Strategic Misguidance," *Physics Today* 39, no. 2 (February 1986): 97–8.

10 Barry M. Goldwater, *With No Apologies* (New York: William Morrow 1979), 299.

11 Eugene V. Rostow, "The Soviet Threat to Europe through the Middle East," in Robert Conquest et al., *Defending America* (New York: Basic Books 1977), 63–4.

12 Roger Speed, *Strategic Deterrence in the 1980s* (Stanford CA: Hoover Institution Press 1979), 15–16.

13 Eugene V. Rostow, "Introduction," to Raymond A. Shulstad, *Peace Is My Profession: A Soldier's View of the Moral Dimension of US Nuclear Policy* (Washington DC: National Defense University Press 1986), xx.

14 Eugene V. Rostow, "Of Summitry and Grand Strategy," *Strategic Review* 14, no. 4 (fall 1986): 14.

15 Norman Podhoretz, *The Present Danger* (New York: Simon and Schuster 1980), 56.

16 Robert C. McFarlane, "Effective Strategic Policy," *Foreign Affairs* 67, no. 1 (fall 1988): 34.

17 Caspar Weinberger, letter of 13 July 1983, in the *New York Review of Books*, 18 August 1983, 30.

18 *New York Times*, 22 January 1985, 7.

19 George F. Will, "The Illusion of Arms Control," *Newsweek*, 13 October 1986, 102.

20 *New York Times*, 20 September 1988, 27.

21 Caspar W. Weinberger, "U.S. Defense Strategy," *Foreign Affairs* 64, no. 4 (spring 1986): 675.

22 Quoted in Philip A.G. Sabin, *Shadow or Substance? Perceptions and Symbolism in Nuclear Force Planning*, Adelphi Paper 222 (London: International Institute for Strategic Studies, summer 1987), 39. See also the discussion and evidence in Steven Kull, *Minds at War: Nuclear Reality and the Inner Conflicts of Defense Policymakers* (New York: Basic Books 1988), 114–26.

23 Robert Komer, "U.S. Defense Strategy," in Joseph Kruzel, ed., *American Defense Annual 1986–87* (Lexington MA: Lexington Books 1986), 38.

24 James Schlesinger, "The Eagle and the Bear: Ruminations on Forty Years of Superpower Relations," *Foreign Affairs* 63, no. 5 (summer 1985): 956–7.

25 Richard Halloran, "Old Dispute on the MX Erupts Anew," *New York Times*, 21 December 1986, E4.

26 Ibid., 23 November 1988, 11. See also Michael Brower, "In Search of the Elusive Stealth Bomber," *Technology Review* 92, no. 4 (May/June 1989), 43.

27 Quoted in Bruce G. Blair, *Strategic Command and Control: Redefining the Nuclear Threat* (Washington DC: Brookings Institution 1985), 29.

28 *New York Times*, 22 January 1985, 7.

29 Robert W. Tucker, "Reagan's Foreign Policy," *Foreign Affairs* 68, no. 1 (America and the World 1988/89): 22.

30 *New York Times*, 24 March 1983, A20.

31 Scheer, *With Enough Shovels*, 232–3.

32 Gregg Herken, "The Earthly Origins of Star Wars," *BAS* 43 (October 1987): 20–8.

33 *New York Times*, 24 March 1983, A20.

34 Ibid., 5 February 1986, 10.

35 William Liscum Borden, *There Will Be No Time: The Revolution in Strategy* (New York: Macmillan 1946), 58 and 163.

36 Caspar W. Weinberger, "Why Offense Needs Defense," *Foreign Policy*, no. 68 (fall 1987): 18.

37 Mortimer B. Zuckerman, "Why This Summit Was a Success," *U.S. News & World Report*, 27 October 1986, 74.

38 As well as Herken, "The Earthly Origins of Star Wars," see Philip M. Boffey et al., *Claiming the Heavens: The 'New York Times' Complete Guide to the Star Wars Debate* (New York: Times Books 1988), chap. 1; Frances FitzGerald, "Memoirs of the Reagan Era," *New Yorker*, 16 January 1989, 90; Newhouse, *War and Peace in the Nuclear Age*, 359–63; Smith, *Power Game*, 603–16; and Talbott, *Master of the Game*, chap. 9.

39 Elizabeth Drew, *Campaign Journal: The Political Events of 1983–1984* (New York: Macmillan 1985), 49.

40 Quoted in Kull, *Minds at War*, 235–6.

41 Daniel O. Graham, *The Non-Nuclear Defense of Cities: The High Frontier Space-Based Defense against ICBM Attack* (Cambridge MA: Abt Books 1983), 1 (emphasis added).

42 Norman Podhoretz, "Arms Control Illusions," *New York Times*, 24 January 1985, 23 (emphasis added).

43 Zbigniew Brzezinski, "To Be Treated like a Great Power, Act like One," *International Herald Tribune*, 11 August 1987, 4 (emphasis added).

44 James R. Schlesinger, "Rhetoric and Realities in the Star Wars Debate," *International Security* 10, no. 1 (summer 1985): 6.

45 Richard Nixon, *1999: Victory without War* (New York: Simon and Schuster 1988), 47.

46 Edward Teller, *Better a Shield than a Sword* (New York: Free Press 1987), 227–8.

47 See, for example, Jonathan Samuel Lockwood, *The Soviet View of U.S. Strategic Doctrine* (New Brunswick NJ: Transaction Books 1985), 176–83.

48 Schlesinger, "Rhetoric and Realities," 3.

49 In offering this discussion, I am indebted to the work of Martha J. Smith, "The Debate over Strategic Defenses, 1967–1987: A Study of American Ideology and Perspectives on National Security" (MA thesis, Queen's University, 1988), chaps. 1 and 2 and pp 80–1.

50 Hedrick Smith, head of the Washington bureau of the *New York Times*, offered an interesting reflection on the president's commitment to SDI. "In personal contact," he remarked, "Reagan is unfailingly cheerful, gracious, polite; he makes people feel good. But to a reporter – and to senators and congressmen – he can sound wooden and staged at close quarters. I have interviewed him several times, all but once with frustration. His answers sounded like replays of a human cassette, his lines rehearsed, even the little jokes. He seemed to be reading a part." Smith then recalled the exception to these tightly scripted encounters. "But once in 1985, by a roaring fire in the Oval Office, I felt a real Reagan. He was talking about his dream of strategic defense, and his tone of voice, his animation, his body language conveyed how deeply he felt. As he leaned into his answers, I gained a sense of his own passion and conviction in a way I would never forget. After that interview, his refusal to compromise on strategic defense ... came as no surprise to me." (*Power Game*, 428–9)

51 Boffey et al., *Claiming the Heavens*, chap. 11.

52 William J. Broad, "Star Wars Is Coming, but Where Is It Going?" *New York Times Magazine*, 6 December 1987, 88. See also Boffey et al., *Claiming the Heavens*, 141–2; and Jack Manno, *Arming the Heavens: The Hidden Military Agenda for Space, 1945–1995* (New York: Dodd, Mead 1984), 2.

53 Lieutenant Colonel Dino A. Lorenzini and Major Charles L. Fox, "2001: A U.S. Space Force," *Naval War College Review* 34, no. 2 (March-April 1981): 64. See also Fred Hiatt, "Air Force Manual Seeks Space Superiority," *Washington Post*, 15 January 1985, A13.

54 Quoted in Thomas Karas, *The New High Ground: Systems and Weapons of Space Age War* (New York: Simon and Schuster 1983), 24 (emphasis added).

55 Edward C. Aldridge, Jr, "The Myths of the Militarization of Space," *International Security* 11, no. 4 (spring 1987): 156.

56 *New York Times*, 14 February 1988, E22. See also Broad's report, "U.S. Is Committed to Nuclear Tests," *New York Times*, 18 October 1987, 1 and 32.

57 Teller, *Better a Shield than a Sword*; Weinberger, "Why Offense Needs Defense," 14–15.

58 Kull, *Minds at War*, 211–12 and 219.

59 Robert W. Tucker, "The Nuclear Debate," *Foreign Affairs* 63, no. 1 (fall 1984): 27.

60 Colin S. Gray, "Space Arms Control: A Skeptical View," *Air University Review* 37, no. 1 (November-December 1985), 84–5. See also Kevin N. Lewis, "Implications for Strategic Offensive Force Modernization," in Samuel F. Wells, Jr, and Robert S. Litwak, eds., *Strategic Defenses and Soviet-American Relations* (Cambridge MA: Ballinger 1987), 79–99.

61 Fred C. Iklé, "Nuclear Strategy: Can There Be a Happy Ending?" *Foreign Affairs* 63, no. 4 (spring 1985), 824–5.

62 Fred C. Iklé, "The Idol of Stability," *National Interest*, no. 6 (winter 1986/87): 76.

63 Kull, *Minds at War*, 236.

64 A useful summary of SDI's history in the 1980s is presented in chapter 10 of Fen Osler Hampson, *Unguided Missiles: How America Buys Its Weapons* (New York: Norton 1989). See also Peter Clausen and Michael Brower, "The Confused Course of SDI," *Technology Review* 90, no. 7 (October 1987): 60–72; Joseph Romm, "Pseudo-Science and SDI," *Arms Control Today* 19, no. 8 (October 1989): 15–21; and Sanford Lakoff and Herbert F. York, *A Shield in Space? Technology, Politics, and the Strategic Defense Initiative* (Berkeley and Los Angeles: University of California Press 1989).

65 George P. Shultz, "New Realities and New Ways of Thinking," *Foreign Affairs* 63, no. 4 (spring 1985); 720.

66 Kenneth L. Adelman, "To Geneva, with Firmness," *New York Times*, 19 January 1987, 17 (emphasis added).

67 Iklé, "The Idol of Stability," 78.

68 Richard Nixon, *Real Peace* (Boston: Little, Brown 1984), 104.

69 Sidney Blumenthal, *The Rise of the Counter-Establishment: From Conservative Ideology to Political Power* (New York: Times Books 1986), 241–2. There are also points of interest in Paul D. Erickson, *Reagan Speaks: The Making of an American Myth* (New York: New York University Press 1985).

70 Frances FitzGerald, "Reflections (Foreign Policy)," *New Yorker*, 11 November 1985, 113.

71 Benjamin R. Barber, "Celluloid Vistas," *Harper's* (July 1985): 74–5.

72 Tucker, "Reagan's Foreign Policy," 26–7.
73 See, for example, William Pfaff, "Reflections (Symbolism in Foreign Policy)," *New Yorker*, 15 September 1986, 102–6.
74 Stanley Hoffmann, "Semidetached Politics," *New York Review of Books*, 8 November 1984, 36.
75 Elizabeth Drew, "Letter from Washington," *New Yorker*, 27 October 1986, 126.
76 "The Talk of the Town," *New Yorker*, 14 November 1988, 32.
77 William Schneider, "'Rambo' and Reality: Having It Both Ways," in Oye, Lieber, and Rothchild, eds., *Eagle Resurgent?* 66 and 71.
78 McGeorge Bundy, *Danger and Survival: Choices about the Bomb in the First Fifty Years* (New York: Random House 1988), 583 (emphasis added).

CHAPTER FOUR

1 Dennis Lee, *The Difficulty of Living on Other Planets* (Toronto: Macmillan 1987), 84–5.
2 *FRUS, 1950*, vol. 1 (1977), 29.
3 Ibid., 30.
4 Robert E. Osgood, *The Nuclear Dilemma in American Strategic Thought* (Boulder CO: Westview 1988), xiii ("Foreword" by Robert W. Tucker) and 41; and James Schlesinger, "Reykjavik and Revelations: A Turn of the Tide?" *Foreign Affairs* 65, no. 3 (America and the World 1986): 429–30.
5 Charles Krauthammer, "On Nuclear Morality," in R. James Woolsey, ed., *Nuclear Arms: Ethics, Strategy, Politics* (San Francisco: Institute for Contemporary Studies 1984), 15.
6 Jacob Viner made a prediction to this effect in "The Implications of the Atomic Bomb for International Relations," *Proceedings of the American Philosophical Society* 90, no. 1 (January 1946): 57.
7 Herbert F. York, *Making Weapons, Talking Peace: A Physicist's Odyssey from Hiroshima to Geneva* (New York: Basic Books 1987), 26.
8 Here I am largely reproducing the argument of Robert L. Holmes, a philosopher, in a letter to the *New York Times*, 17 January 1988, E26.
9 Adam Ulam, *Expansion and Coexistence: Soviet Foreign Policy, 1917–73*, 2nd ed. (New York: Praeger 1974), 497.
10 Morton H. Halperin, *Nuclear Fallacy: Dispelling the Myth of Nuclear Strategy* (Cambridge MA: Ballinger 1987), chap. 2.
11 Robert L. Messer, "New Evidence on Truman's Decision," *BAS* 41 (August 1985): 50–6.
12 Rosemary J. Foot, "Nuclear Coercion and the Ending of the Korean Conflict," *International Security* 13, no. 3 (winter 1988/89): 92–112; and

McGeorge Bundy, *Danger and Survival: Choices about the Bomb in the First Fifty Years* (New York: Random House 1988), 238–45.

13 Gordon H. Chang, "To the Nuclear Brink: Eisenhower, Dulles, and the Quemoy-Matsu Crisis," *International Security* 12, no. 4 (spring 1988): 122–2; Foot, "Ending of the Korean Conflict," 112; and John Wilson Lewis and Xue Litai, *China Builds the Bomb* (Stanford CA: Stanford University Press 1988), 34–7.

14 Colin S. Gray, *Maritime Strategy, Geopolitics, and the Defense of the West* (New York: National Strategy Information Center 1986), 17–18.

15 These issues are examined in an excellent article by Michael MccGwire, "Deterrence: the Problem – Not the Solution," *International Affairs* 62, no. 1 (winter 1985/86): 55–70.

16 Even before nuclear weapons existed, one astute observer was already conceiving the most likely scenario of a war between the United States and the Soviet Union. In a book published in 1944, when these two powers were still formal allies, William T.R. Fox suggested that the "danger is probably not so much that either power will deliberately and directly seek conflict with the other, since the evidence is so clear that such a conflict would be a catastrophe to both, in terms of the values which each pursues. Victory over the other, even if it could be attained, and that is itself doubtful, would involve the sacrifice of other values for the loss of which military victory would hardly compensate. The greater danger is that they will be drawn into a third world war *indirectly* or *reluctantly* – indirectly by finding themselves in a conflict which is not at first a Soviet-American war, or reluctantly by the leadership in one country coming to be convinced that conflict with the other is 'inevitable'." This scenario lost none of its plausibility after 1945. (*The Super-Powers: The United States, Britain, and the Soviet Union* [New York: Harcourt, Brace 1944], 99–100.)

17 Richard Ned Lebow, "Provocative Deterrence: A New Look at the Cuban Missile Crisis," *Arms Control Today* 18, no. 6 (July/August 1988): 15–16.

18 Robert V. Daniels, *Russia: The Roots of Confrontation* (Cambridge MA: Harvard University Press 1985), 345.

19 United Kingdom, Public Record Office, FO 371, nos. 135241 (NS. 1021/31) and 135242 (NS 1021/53), both from 1958. See also the speech by Sidney E. Smith, the Canadian secretary of state for external affairs, "Peacemaking: Fission and Fusion, part 2," in Department of External Affairs, Statements and Speeches 58/42, 29 October 1958, 13.

20 Arkady N. Shevchenko, *Breaking with Moscow* (New York: Knopf 1985), 83–4.

21 Matthew Evangelista, *Innovation and the Arms Race: How the United States and the Soviet Union Develop New Military Technologies* (Ithaca NY: Cornell University Press 1988), 265; see in general 262–7.

22 Thomas B. Cochran, William M. Arkin, and Milton M. Hoenig, *Nuclear Weapons Databook.* 1: *U.S. Nuclear Forces and Capabilities* (Cambridge MA: Ballinger 1984), 15. In an article written just before the Cuban crisis, Michael Brower wondered about some of the implications for Soviet policy of the strenuous American pursuit of nuclear superiority (the "missile gap" had by then been acknowledged to be non-existent). "What is the impact," he asked, "of our drive for nuclear supremacy on the relative power of the contending forces within the Soviet Union and other communist countries? Will it strengthen the hands of those arguing for limitations on the arms race, for more spending on housing, agriculture, and consumer goods, for reaching at least limited accommodation with the West, for going slow on Berlin, for striving for disarmament and accepting some limitations on Soviet secrecy and sovereignty in order to get it? Or will our policy tend instead to strengthen the power of those who believe that the 'imperialist powers' are preparing for war, that ultimately war between the two ideologies is inevitable, that the communists must prepare for this war, and that meaningful negotiations and accommodations with the West are impossible or dangerous?" ("Nuclear Strategy of the Kennedy Administration," *BAS* 18 [October 1962]: 41.) A letter from J. David Singer published in response to this article offered a pertinent comment on the claim that negotiations with the other side were only possible from a position of strength: "The Kennedy administration is not interested in launching a first strike. But it is very interested in looking as if it might (to the Soviets, not the neutrals). That way, the Soviets may be induced to return to the bargaining table as a chastened and docile supplicant. But the expectation is naive. Having this great strategic preponderance, we won't have to negotiate, and the Soviets will be afraid to." (*BAS* 19 [February 1963]: 35.) This was a sound assessment. Negotiations for arms control only became serious a few years later, when a rough equality of nuclear power had been reached.

23 Sir John Slessor, "The Great Deterrent and Its Limitations," *BAS* 12 (May 1956): 149.

24 Henry L. Roberts, *Russia and America: Dangers and Prospects* (New York: Harper for the Council on Foreign Relations 1956), 110.

25 York, *Making Weapons, Talking Peace,* 26 (emphasis added); cf. Vannevar Bush, *Pieces of the Action* (New York: William Morrow 1970), 63.

26 Joseph S. Nye, Jr, "International Security Studies," in Joseph Kruzel, ed., *American Defense Annual 1988–1989* (Lexington MA: Lexington Books 1988), 238.

27 McGeorge Bundy, "Existential Deterrence and Its Consequences," in Douglas MacLean, ed., *The Security Gamble: Deterrence Dilemmas in the Nuclear Age* (Totowa NJ: Rowan and Allanheld 1984), 7–8.

28 Bundy, *Danger and Survival*, 616–17.

29 Larry D. Welch, "Foreword" to Richard H. Kohn and Joseph P. Hara-han, eds., *Strategic Air Warfare: An Interview with Generals Curtis E. LeMay, Leon W. Johnson, David A. Burchinal, and Jack J. Catton* (Washington DC: United States Air Force 1988), v.

30 Russell E. Dougherty, "The Psychological Climate of Nuclear Command," in Ashton B. Carter, John D. Steinbruner, and Charles A. Zraket, eds., *Managing Nuclear Operations* (Washington DC: Brookings Institution 1987), 422.

31 Carroll L. Zimmerman, *Insider at SAC: Operations Analysis under General LeMay* (Manhattan KA: Sunflower University Press 1988), 103 and 115.

32 D. Douglas Dalgleish and Larry Schweikart, *Trident* (Carbondale and Edwardsville IL: Southern Illinois University Press 1984), 372.

33 John M. Weinstein, "NATO Should Modernize Its Nuclear Artillery," *Arms Control Today* 19, no. 2 (March 1989): 28.

34 David Holloway, *The Soviet Union and the Arms Race* (New Haven CT: Yale University Press 1983), 71–2; and Michael MccGwire, *Military Objectives in Soviet Foreign Policy* (Washington DC: Brookings Institution 1987), 78–9.

35 Zbigniew Brzezinski, *Power and Principle: Memoirs of the National Security Adviser 1977–1981* (New York: Farrar, Straus, Groux 1983), 457.

36 Hans J. Morgenthau, "Decisionmaking in the Nuclear Age," *BAS* 18 (December 1962): 7.

37 *Discriminate Deterrence: Report of the Commission on Integrated Long-Term Strategy* (Washington DC, January 1988).

38 Zbigniew Brzezinski, "America's New Geostrategy," *Foreign Affairs* 66, no. 4 (spring 1988): 681 and 683. Similar claims were made by Albert Wohlstetter and Richard Brody, "Continuing Control as a Requirement for Deterring," in Ashton Carter et al., eds., *Managing Nuclear Operations*, 168–9, and by Fred S. Hoffman, "SDI, Threats of Indiscriminate Destruction, and Stability in East-West Relations," in Brent Scowcroft, R. James Woolsey, and Thomas H. Etzold, eds., *Defending Peace and Freedom: Toward Strategic Stability in the Year 2000* (Lanham MD: University Press of America 1988), 163. There were striking similarities between these arguments and those of Henry Kissinger some thirty years before in his *Nuclear Weapons and Foreign Policy* (1957).

39 Brzezinski, "America's New Geostrategy," 685.

40 "Reflections on the Quarter," *Orbis* 4, no. 1 (spring 1960): 3.

41 Solly Zuckerman, *Monkeys, Men and Missiles: An Autobiography 1946–88* (London: Collins 1988), 307.

42 Quoted in R. Jeffrey Smith, "Reassessment Takes Glow out of Soviet Arms Offer," *International Herald Tribune*, 2 October 1989, 4.

43 William M. Arkin and Richard W. Fieldhouse, *Nuclear Battlefields: Global Links in the Arms Race* (Cambridge MA: Ballinger 1985), xvi–xvii.

44 Alan L. Gropman, "The Thirst for Nuclear Awareness," *Strategic Review* 17, no. 2 (spring 1989): 68.

45 Richard P. Stebbins, *The United States in World Affairs, 1953* (New York: Harper for the Council on Foreign Relations 1955), 354. A similar point was being made thirty years later in Arkin and Fieldhouse, *Nuclear Battlefields*, 144–5; see also Janne E. Nolan, *Guardians of the Arsenal: The Politics of Nuclear Strategy* (New York: Basic Books 1989), 30–3.

46 Morgenthau, "Decisionmaking in the Nuclear Age," 8. Writing in 1987, an American military scientist with government service, including work with the Joint Strategic Target Planning Staff (which prepared nuclear war plans), gave voice to this sort of insider's sense of special expertise and authority. Reviewing a book on the control of nuclear weapons, he asserted that "an accurate understanding" of the management of nuclear weapons "demands the most specialized as well as practical knowledge and credentials ... More important, it entails the most sensitive information bearing upon the security of the United States and its allies. In short, an accurate and comprehensive treatment of the subject could not be published in the open literature." He asked: "How can scholars, even with the best of intentions, hope to produce an authoritative book on this subject?" Such claims of exclusive knowledge, though often implicit, were not usually presented quite as brazenly as this. (N.F. Wikner, "How Well Controlled Are Our Nuclear Arms?" *Strategic Review* 15, no. 2 [spring 1987]: 75.)

47 Among the sources that bear on these matters are the following: Shaun Gregory and Alistair Edwards, "The Hidden Cost of Deterrence: Nuclear Weapons Accidents 1950–88," *Bulletin of Peace Proposals* 20, no. 1 (March 1989): 3–26; William M. Arkin and Joshua M. Handler, "Nuclear Disasters at Sea, Then and Now," *BAS* 45 (July/August 1989): 20–4; Keith Schneider, "How Secrecy on Atomic Weapons Helped Breed a Policy of Disregard," *New York Times*, 13 November 1988, E7; Keith Schneider, "The Soviets Show Scars from Nuclear Arms Production," *New York Times*, 16 July 1989, E2; Deborah Blum, "Weird Science: Livermore's X-Ray Laser Flap," *BAS* 44 (July/August 1988): 7–13; Richard H. Ullman, "The Covert French Connection," *Foreign Policy*, no. 75 (summer 1989): 3–33; and (regarding launch on warning) *BAS* 45 (May 1989): 2–3.

48 Molly Moore, "Harder View in U.S. Imperils New Arms," *International Herald Tribune*, 4 July 1989, 3.

49 Elmo R. Zumwalt, Jr, "Seapower," in Joseph Kruzel, ed., *American Defense Annual 1987–1988* (Lexington MA: Lexington Books 1987), 122.

50 See, for example, the reflections of General Russell E. Dougherty, a former commander-in-chief of SAC (1974–7), in his essay, "The Psychological Climate of Nuclear Command," 420.

51 Mikhail Gorbachev, *Perestroika: New Thinking for Our Country and the World* (New York: Harper and Row 1987), 11–12.
52 Ibid., 142.
53 Mikhail Gorbachev, "Time to Discard Illusions," *Manchester Guardian Weekly*, 18 December 1988, 12.
54 Gorbachev, *Perestroika*, 141.
55 Ibid., 140.
56 Ibid., 146–7.
57 Ibid., 141. Among the most thoughtful of the early assessments of Gorbachev's policies, in the late 1980s, were: Stephen M. Meyer, "The Sources and Prospects of Gorbachev's New Political Thinking on Security," *International Security* 13, no. 2 (fall 1988): 124–63; Bruce Parrott, "Soviet National Security under Gorbachev," *Problems of Communism*, 37, no. 6 (November-December 1988): 1–36; and David Holloway, "State, Society, and the Military under Gorbachev," *International Security* 14, no. 2 (winter 1989/90): 5–24.
58 *FRUS, 1952–54*, vol. II, part 2 (1984), 1073.
59 Anatol Rapoport, *Strategy and Conscience* (New York: Harper and Row 1964), 286.
60 William E. Odom, "Soviet Military Doctrine," *Foreign Affairs* 67, no. 2 (winter 1988/89): 131.
61 Richard P. Stebbins, *The United States in World Affairs, 1950* (New York: Harper for the Council on Foreign Relations 1951), 158–9 and 64.
62 Niels Bohr, "Open Letter to the United Nations, 9 June 1950," in A.P. French and P.J. Kennedy, eds., *Niels Bohr: A Centenary Volume* (Cambridge MA: Harvard University Press 1985), 294.
63 Rusty Schweickart, "Our Backs against the Bomb, Our Eyes on the Stars," *Discover* 8, no. 7 (July 1987), 62.

EPILOGUE

1 Marie Vassiltchikov, *Berlin Diaries, 1940–1945* (New York: Knopf 1987), 149.
2 James Gleick, "After the Bomb, a Mushroom Cloud of Metaphors," *New York Times Book Review*, 21 May 1989, 53.
3 Robert W. Gardiner, *The Cool Arm of Destruction: Modern Weapons and Moral Insensitivity* (Philadelphia PA: Westminster Press 1974), 141 and 29.
4 Thomas C. Schelling and Morton H. Halperin, *Strategy and Arms Control* (New York: Twentieth Century Fund 1961), 5.
5 Stanley Hoffmann, "Realism and Its Discontents," *Atlantic* (November 1985): 136 (first emphasis added).

Index